lonely 🌐 planet

POCKET

PORTLAND & THE WILLAMETTE VALLEY

TOP EXPERIENCES • LOCAL LIFE

CELESTE BRASH, MASOVAIDA MORGAN

Contents

Plan Your Trip 4

Skidmore Fountain (p60)
BENEDEK/GETTY IMAGES ©

COVID-19

We have re-checked every business in this book before publication to ensure that it is still open after the COVID-19 outbreak. However, the economic and social impacts of COVID-19 will continue to be felt long after the outbreak has been contained, and many businesses, services and events referenced in this guide may experience ongoing restrictions. Some businesses may be temporarily closed, have changed their opening hours and services, or require bookings; some unfortunately could have closed permanently. We suggest you check with venues before visiting for the latest information.

Top Experiences

ARTYOORAN/SHUTTERSTOCK ©

Explore Pioneer Courthouse Square

Settle into Portland's living room. **p32**

CHRIS ANSON/SHUTTERSTOCK ©

Stroll by the River at Tom McCall Waterfront Park

An emerald esplanade of activity. **p30**

BENEDEK-GETTY IMAGES ©

Check Out Local Culture at Alberta Arts District

Portland's multi-cultural creative hub. **p84**

Browse the Stacks at Powell's City of Books

A city block of books. **p68**

C. ECHEVESTE/SHUTTERSTOCK ©

Sample Craft Beer in Beervana
Best for Beervana's unique brews. **p102**

Find Handcrafted Souvenirs at Saturday Market

Portland's bizarre local bazaar. **p54**

Relax at Tranquil Lan Su Chinese Garden

An oasis of Chinese traditions. **p52**

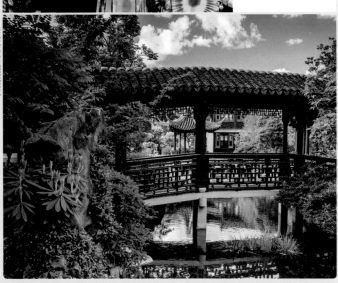

Hike Urban Trails at Forest Park

An enchanting urban wilderness. **p80**

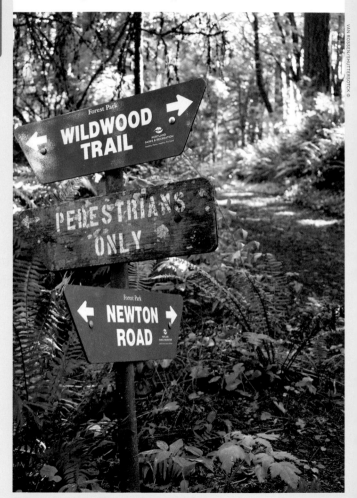

VAN ROSSEN/SHUTTERSOTCK ©

Forest Park
WILDWOOD TRAIL

PEDESTRIANS ONLY

Forest Park
NEWTON ROAD

STEVE ESTVANIK/SHUTTERSTOCK ©

Enjoy the Greenery at Washington Park

An idyllic hillside retreat. **p48**

Discover Columbia River Gorge

Waterfalls, forests and a mighty big river. **p116**

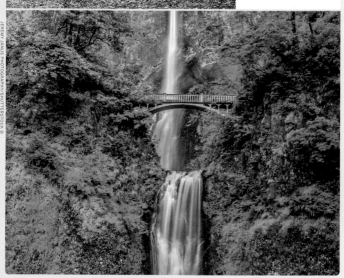

JEREMY JANUS PHOTOGRAPHY/SHUTTERSTOCK ©

Dining Out

Expect everything from food carts and fast casual joints to upmarket establishments and experimental, multicourse eateries. The city's chefs have an arsenal of fresh, seasonal ingredients – meaning even the most humble dishes are top quality.

Street Food

Some of Portland's most amazing food comes from humble little kitchens-on-wheels. Found all over town clumped together in parking lots or otherwise un-occupied spaces, food carts offer hungry wanderers a chance to try unusual dishes at low prices, and they often have covered seating areas if you don't like to walk while you eat. Many of Portland's beloved eateries got their start as food carts, with specialties that were such hits that brick-and-mortar locations were established to serve increasing demands.

Brunch

Portlanders love brunch and are willing to wait in long lines to get it. At the most popular places, it's not unheard of to arrive when the restaurant opens and learn that you face a two-hour wait. Weekend hours are usually from 9am to 2pm; some places are open only Satur-day and Sunday.

Fine Dining

Portland is nationally recognized for its food scene, with dozens of young, top-notch chefs pushing the boundaries of ethnic and regional cuisines and making the most of locally sourced, sustainably raised ingredients. Fairly casual clothes are acceptable even at higher-end places, where reservations are a good idea.

Best Brunch

Screen Door Withstand the infamous queue and then reward yourself with

DEE BROWNING/SHUTTERSTOCK ©

Southern-fried goodness like chicken and waffles. (p99)

Pine State Biscuits Mammoth Southern-style biscuit breakfast sandwiches with decadent adornments like fried chicken. (p91)

Best Upmarket

Le Pigeon Portland's favorite French restaurant offers a comprehensive experience with a seven-course tasting menu. (p111)

Imperial Renowned chef Vitaly Paley nails new American cuisine at this upscale hotel joint. (p44)

Best International Fare

Akadi PDX Authentic West African dishes prepared by a chef from the Ivory Coast. (p91)

Kachka Traditional Russian dishes served with a side of Soviet kitsch in this homey space. (p110)

Best Pacific Northwest Cuisine

Higgins A Portland institution, this elegant downtown

eatery has been serving PNW classics since 1994. (p44)

Beast Thoughtfully sourced ingredients enjoy adventurous execution across six courses on this prix-fixe menu. (p92)

Irving Street Kitchen Pacific Northwest shareables with a Southern touch, served in an urban-rustic space. (p77)

Bar Open

Drinking, whether it's coffee or a craft brew, cider, cocktail or kombucha, is practically a sport in Portland. In winter it's a reason to hunker down and escape the rain; in summer, an excuse to sit on a patio or deck and soak up the long-awaited sunshine.

AGAVE PHOTO STUDIO/SHUTTERSTOCK ©

Beervana

Portland was an early adopter of the craft-beer craze. Several of the industry's pioneers are still going strong, like the ubiquitous McMenamins, but new breweries crop up every year and most are well worth checking out. If you know what you like, you'll surely find it, as even dive-ish bars tend to have a pretty good tap list; if you're not sure what you want, head to any brewery and try a flight of different offerings.

Or just ask questions: most servers are well versed in what they're pouring and happy to offer tastes and make recommendations.

Coffee Paradise

Portland is full of excellent artisan coffee shops that take their roasting and brewing seriously. Even at average places, baristas know their stuff; your pour-over might take a while to get to you, but it'll be one of the best in your life. If you're a huge coffee buff or just eager to learn, try to attend a

cupping session, or ask at a local shop about special tastings.

Cocktail Heaven

The 'bar' is as high for creative cocktails in Portland as it is for beer and coffee. Watering holes range from seedy dives to classy lounges.

Best Brews

Breakside Brewery
Experimental brews spiked with fruits, vegetables and spices, plus an award-winning IPA. (p77)

Hopworks Urban Brewery
All-organic beers made with local ingredients. (p112)

MICHAEL GORDON/SHUTTERSTOCK ©

Laurelwood Brewing Co Kid-friendly brewpub with organic suds on tap. (p94)

Ecliptic Brewing Ambitious ales and IPAs named after the cosmos. (p94)

Cascade Brewing Barrel House Specializes in sour beers, many of which are fruit-based. (p112)

Best Coffee

Proud Mary Aussie-based roaster with stellar java and Insta-worthy brunch plates. (p93)

Barista This tiny sliver of a cafe was one of Portland's original third-wave coffee shops. (p77)

Push x Pull Bright, cheery shop with natural-process coffees and superfriendly staff. (p111)

Deadstock Coffee Sneaker-themed joint owned by a Nike janitor turned designer. (p63)

Stumptown Coffee Roasters This Portland roasting empire started with one roastery and cafe in 1999 and helped small-batch roasting go mainstream. (pictured; p63)

Best Cocktails

Abigail Hall Historic hotel bar with cozy, retro vibes and large-format libations. (p44)

Hey Love Hip hotel bar with tropical vibes, slinging tiki-themed cocktails and boozy slushies. (p113)

Scotch Lodge Cozy, subterranean lounge with some 300 whiskeys and Scotch-centric cocktails. (p111)

Departure Lounge Super swanky eatery and cocktail bar with stellar views from the rooftop of a downtown luxury hotel. (p45)

Treasure Hunt

Part of the excitement of shopping in Portland is that there's no sales tax. That combined with a number of indie shops around town that celebrate locally produced goods can make for a fun retail experience.

KENNSTILGER47/SHUTTERSTOCK ©

Books & Music

The largest independent bookstore in the country, Powell's City of Books spans an entire block and contains more than a million titles. But there are plenty of other indie bookstores around town as well as fun-to-browse record stores.

Wine & Weed

Portland has well over 300 pot dispensaries and more seem to be opening by the day since cannabis went legal in 2014. Not into weed? The local wines are world class. Of course everything in the city is sold with a creative twist.

Best Book & Music Shops

Powell's City of Books A whole city block of books – new, used, rare, small-press, special-edition, out-of-print and more. (p68)

Music Millennium This venerable record store with new and used selections is the oldest in the Pacific Northwest. (p115)

Floating World Comics Well-curated collection of comics and graphic novels, spanning multiple genres. (p65)

Tender Loving Empire Hip concept shop and music label with an in-store listening booth and records for sale. (p47)

Broadway Books Indie bookstore with solid nonfiction, biography and literary-fiction sections, plus regular author readings. (p97)

Best Wine & Weed Shops

Thelonius Wines Natural and organic wines are the focus at this shop that doubles as a tasting room. (p79)

Green Hop Hip-hop themed dispensary with strains named after artists who sing the praises of cannabis. (p87)

Pairings Select a bottle of organic wine based on your star sign or favorite rock song. (p115)

HEATH KORVOLA/GETTY IMAGES ©

Uplift Botanicals Friendly dispensary with knowledgeable budtenders and daily rotating specials. (p96)

Best Clothing & Accessories

Kiriko Made Atelier using vintage Japanese textiles to create clothes and accessories with ages-old techniques. (p64)

Frock Boutique Bright, cheery clothing and accessories by independent designers. (p97)

Next Adventure Score deals on sportswear and adventure gear in this outdoor store's 'bargain basement'. (p115)

Laundry Throwback streetwear from the '80s and '90s. (p64)

Orox Leather Goods Fine leather bags and accessories are handmade in this family-run workshop and showroom. (p64)

Ray's Ragtime High-quality vintage threads, mostly spanning the '40s through '70s. (p96)

Best Gifts

MadeHere PDX Goods of some 280 PNW-based vendors are showcased in this expansive Pearl District space. (p78)

Flutter Curio shop that reclaims and charmingly curates found objects, vintage wares and would-be clutter. (p97)

ZimZim Pop-culture novelties, T-shirts, birthday cards, tchotchkes and other quirky treasures. (p115)

Saturday Market

The largest and longest-running open-air craft market in the US, Portland's Saturday Market (p54) is home to hundreds of vendors, which are all chosen by a jury. Despite the name, it's open on Sundays, too.

Outdoors

Home to the nation's largest urban park, Portland's outdoor spaces range from vast and wild to manicured and contained. Wherever you find yourself, Portland's scenery stays green pretty much year-round. You can thank the rain later – and never let it deter you from getting outside.

TERENCELEEZY/GETTY IMAGES ©

Best Hiking

Forest Park The largest urban park in the US, with trails totaling 150 miles. (p80)

Hoyt Arboretum Twelve miles of trails span this garden in Washington Park. (p49)

Columbia River Gorge Less than an hour's drive from Portland, hikers are spoiled in the gorge. (p116)

Silver Falls State Park Loop through waterfall-filled forests in this huge state park near Salem. (pictured; p144)

Best Gardens

Japanese Garden A traditional teahouse, sand garden and koi ponds set a wonderfully zen scene. (p49)

Crystal Springs Rhododendron Garden Rhododendrons and azaleas reach peak bloom in May and stick around all summer. (p108)

Lan Su Chinese Garden Tranquil garden with a plant scavenger hunt guide. (p52)

Best Views

Pittock Mansion Unparalleled panoramas of downtown and Mt Hood from the backyard. (p81)

International Rose Test Garden See Rose City from the eastern edge of its namesake flower garden. (p49)

Best Parks

Tom McCall Waterfront Park A wonderful place to see springtime cherry blossoms. (p30)

Washington Park All-encompassing home to several gardens and cultural attractions. (p48)

Mill Ends Park At 24in in diameter, the world's tiniest park is reputedly home to leprechauns. (p41)

Best Wildlife Spotting

Oaks Bottom Wildlife Refuge Wetland refuge with birdlife such as hawks, coots, kestrels and widgeons. (p108)

Vaux's Swifts Each September, multitudes of Vaux's swifts spiral down a school's brick chimney to roost for the night. (p74)

Show Time

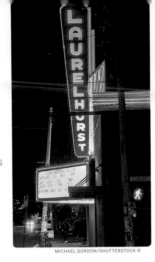

Internationally renowned indie bands put Portland on the map as a musical hot spot, but a deeper look at the city's local entertainment scene reveals a coterie of diverse performers that excel in everything from opera to burlesque and heavy metal to jazz. And don't miss the ambient, independent cinemas that serve food and drink.

MICHAEL GORDON/SHUTTERSTOCK ©

Best Live-Music Venues

Doug Fir Lounge Top indie acts perform in this subterranean, log-cabin-inspired venue and restaurant. (p114)

Mississippi Studios Intimate venue in a former church, with great acts and a fantastic, all-analog sound system. (p95)

Crystal Ballroom Historic venue with a 'floating', bouncy floor that feels like jumping on a trampoline when the house is packed. (p47)

Dante's Atmospheric venue hosting local and touring acts, with late-night pizza on deck. (p46)

Goodfoot Neighborhood joint with affordable basement shows and open-mike Mondays. (p114)

Revolution Hall There isn't a bad seat in the auditorium of this former high school. (p114)

Best Cinemas

Hollywood Theatre Art deco cinema with classic, foreign and indie screenings, plus 70mm capabilities. (p95)

Laurelhurst Theater Primarily first-run flicks that can be enjoyed with pizza, beer and wine. (pictured; p114)

Cinema 21 Single-screen '20s-era theater, showing foreign, art-house and classic films. (p71)

Best Performing Arts

Arlene Schnitzer Concert Hall Historic Italian rococo-style theater that's home to the Oregon Symphony and other cultural performances. (p47)

Keller Auditorium Home to the Portland Opera and the Oregon Ballet Theatre, plus occasional Broadway productions. (p46)

Portland Center Stage Portland's primary theater company, which performs in a state-of-the-art, two-stage landmark space known as the Armory. (p78)

Under the Radar

KEETON GALE/SHUTTERSTOCK ©

In Portland, a little local knowledge will really enhance your experience. This is a city whose charm is primarily experiential, from cool eating districts only locals know to activities and hangouts where you might be the only tourist.

Best in Portland

Common Ground Portlanders love to unwind here with a hot tub soak, sauna and massage. (p87)

Akadi PDX & **Chin's Kitchen** Northeast Portland is where locals go to savor authentic ethnic cuisine. (p91)

Vaux's Swifts Every September, Portlanders gather nightly to watch a flock of birds plummet down an old chimney to roost. (p74)

Cinema 21 Portland's love affair with all things indie extends to avant-garde films at this art-house cinema. (p71)

Hoxton The rooftop bar has great city views, and there's a subterranean speakeasy so covert that it doesn't even have a name. (p62)

Goodfoot Rather than hitting the manic dance floors in Old Town on Friday nights, locals in the southeast cut a rug to old-school soul tracks. (p114)

Forest Park This pastoral retreat on the city's edge is a favorite escape for Portlanders. (p80)

Portland Timbers Portland's Major League Soccer team has a huge, cultlike following and a game is like no other US sports experience. (Timbers Army pictured; www.timbers.com)

Best Places to Explore Further Afield

Corvallis About 85 miles south of Portland you'll find this university town with bakeries, bookstores, cafes and a delightful riverfront area.

Eugene The heartbeat of Oregon's alternative-lifestyle personality with a bubbling art scene, great restaurants and fun festivals; Eugene is about 110 miles from Portland.

Art

ARTRAN/GETTY IMAGES ©

Portlandia-based cliche notions aside, this city possesses an earnest and unbridled creative spirit. It's evident in numerous art galleries and museums, plus a strong 'maker' scene where art goes beyond gallery spaces and museum walls. Take it in with festivals, 'art walks' or DIY endeavors that allow anybody with an itch to create to do so in an encouraging way.

Best Places to Admire Art

Portland Art Museum Portland's premier art museum including a wing solely dedicated to Native American art. (pictured; p41)

Center for Contemporary Art & Culture Pacific Northwest College of Art's space with revolving visual art and design collections. (p74)

Land Gift shop with an upstairs gallery showcasing original works by up-and-coming and established indie artists; the setting of *Portlandia*'s 'Put a Bird on It' sketch. (p96)

Compound Gallery Old Town Chinatown streetwear shop with a gallery dedicated to urban subculture and pop art. (p65)

Maryhill Museum of Art Remarkable museum, spectacularly located on a bluff above the Columbia Gorge, with a collection including sculpture and drawings by Auguste Rodin. (p119)

Hallie Ford Museum of Art Salem's top art museum boasts the state's best collection of Pacific Northwest art. (p144)

Best Art Events

Last Thursday on Alberta Art walk where indie artists and galleries put works on display for the masses. (p85)

First Thursday Art Walk Wander galleries and businesses downtown as they open their doors for new exhibitions. (p42)

Art in the Pearl Each Labor Day weekend, some 100 artists display and sell works at this juried fine arts-and-crafts festival in the Pearl District. (p75)

Best DIY

Pistils Nursery Hosts workshops on terrarium design, bonsai building and more, plus regular 'maker' trunk shows and gallery events. (p97)

Elements Glass Offers glass-blowing classes during the holiday season, when you can make your own Christmas ornaments. (p74)

For Kids

Kids of all ages will have plenty of ways to stay busy in Portland. The city's wealth of parks, playgrounds and outdoor spaces are great for running around, and on rainy days, there are fantastic museums that are as educational as they are entertaining.

ALEXANDER OGANEZOV/SHUTTERSTOCK ©

Best Museums

Portland Children's Museum Has a maze, theater, clay studio and plenty of outdoor play space. (p49)

Oregon Museum of Science & Industry Exhibitions, planetarium, movie theater and a submarine tour for all ages. (p108)

Oregon Historical Society Features a sprawling permanent historical exhibit with hands-on activities and games. (p40)

Best Attractions

Oregon Zoo Primates, penguins and African savanna animals in their own impressive semi-natural habitats. (p49)

Oaks Park Amusement park with go-karts, a roller rink and plenty of rides. (pictured; p115)

PlayDate PDX Castle-themed indoor playground with attractions for kids of all ages (and their parents!) (p74)

Best Rainy-Day Activities

Ground Kontrol Classic Arcade Bi-level arcade bar that welcomes all ages from noon to 5pm daily. (p62)

Powell's City of Books Massive independent bookstore with plenty of picks for kids. (p68)

Kennedy School Theater Second-run flicks in an old elementary school, with infant-friendly 'crybaby matinees'. (p87)

Best Outdoor Activities

Washington Park An expansive park with picnic tables and a playground and home to attractions like the children's museum and the zoo. (p48)

Lan Su Chinese Garden Traditional garden with koi ponds, a plant scavenger hunt and fortune-telling. (p52)

Salmon Street Springs Fountain Riverside fountain with computer-generated jets that are a blast on a sweltering day. (p40)

Japanese Garden Educational tea ceremonies, bonsai tree demos and koto harp performances. (p49)

LGBTIQ+

With one of the highest populations of LGBTIQ+ residents in the US – second only to San Francisco – queer culture is ingrained in Portland's social fabric. Most every place in the city is extremely welcoming and LGBTIQ-friendly, and you'll see rainbow flags posted in the windows and yards of countless businesses and residences.

DIEGO G DIAZ/SHUTTERSTOCK ©

There Goes the Gayborhood

The Old Town Chinatown area has many gay-specific venues, but Portland is so LGBTIQ-friendly that it lacks a definitive 'gayborhood' – so if you're here and you're queer, consider yourself at home. Venues that aren't LGBTIQ-specific host queer-centric events like dance parties, bar nights, cinema series and film festivals. And if nothing directly catering to the community is on at any given place, you can count on the presence of at least a couple of other queer people.

Best LGBTIQ+ Nightlife

Crush Lounge with an especially inclusive atmosphere and events like drag open mics and BPFQ (bi/pan/fluid/queer) nights. (p113)

CC Slaughters Nightclub with a bumping dance floor, complete with a disco ball. (p63)

Silverado In a city that loves its strip clubs, this is the only one exclusively featuring male dancers. (p63)

Best LGBTIQ+ Entertainment

Hollywood Theatre Queer-centric documentary and horror film series, plus a monthly film festival. (p95)

Darcelle XV Vegas-style cabaret drag show, run by Portland's octogenarian drag queen icon. (p64)

Portland Pride One of the biggest pride celebrations on the West Coast, with marches, films, brunches and a big, gay boat ride. (pictured; p31)

Clinton Street Theater The world's longest-running screening of *The Rocky Horror Picture Show*, every Saturday night since 1978. (www.clintonsttheater.com)

Four Perfect Days

Day 1

DAVFALAN/GETTY IMAGES ©

Start on your adventure with a strong cup of coffee from **Barista** (p77). Once you're properly caffeinated, make a pilgrimage to the beloved **Powell's City of Books** (p68), then browse your way through the area on your way to lunch at **Tasty n Alder** (p43), downtown.

Indulge in some people-watching and take a mandatory selfie with the umbrella-holding statue in **Pioneer Courthouse Square** (p32) before wandering **Tom McCall Waterfront Park** (pictured above; p30).

After dinner at **Pine Street Market** (p62), check out the nightlife in Old Town Chinatown. Take in a drag cabaret show at **Darcelle XV** (p64) and then finish up with a nightcap and a round of pinball at **Ground Kontrol** (p62).

Day 2

RANDY RUNTSCH/SHUTTERSTOCK ©

On day two, lace up your hiking boots and take the woodsy trail through **Forest Park** (p80) up to **Pittock Mansion** (p81) to take in the epic view of the city. Have a well-earned lunch at **Olympia Provisions** (p76).

Make your way back up into the hills to **Washington Park** (p48) and its many gardens such as the Japanese Garden (pictured above) and International Rose Test Gardens, before winding your way to Southeast Portland for dinner at **Le Pigeon** (p111).

After dinner, catch a live band at the **Doug Fir Lounge** (p114). Finish the night with drinks under the vines at **Hey Love** (p113).

Day 3

BOB POOL/SHUTTERSTOCK ©

Southeast adventures continue for day three. Rent a bicycle and grab a route map for a two-wheeled, self-guided tour of some of Portland's dozens of craft breweries in the area. Lunch at **Kachka** (p110).

Make your way further east to the Hawthorne District. Pick up a crystal or deck of tarot cards at a hippie shop, or try on some new threads at one of the vintage stores, then settle in for a movie at the **Bagdad Theater** (p114).

Stick around the neighborhood for an aperitif at one of the many restaurant bars, then chow amazing pizza at **Ken's Artisan Pizza** (p110) before dancing at **Goodfoot** (p114).

Day 4

ARTYOORAN/SHUTTERSTOCK ©

Begin your final day in Portland by taking in the exhibits at the **Portland Art Museum** (pictured above; p41) then head to Northeast for lunch at **Akadi PDX** (p91).

Head over to **Alberta Street** (p84) to check out the boutiques, galleries and coffee shops. Stick around for **Last Thursday on Alberta** (p85) if the timing is right, or head over to Mississippi Ave to browse more shops before dinner at **Ox** (p92).

When you finally roll yourself away from the dinner table, see if there's a live band on at **Mississippi Studios** (p95). After that, take your pick from loads of bars along Mississippi Ave, N Williams Ave or Alberta St for a nightcap celebrating your trip.

Need to Know

For detailed information, see Survival Guide p148

Currency
US dollar ($)

Language
English

Money
Portland is full of banks with exchange services and ATMs. Credit cards are accepted at most hotels, stores and restaurants. Farmers markets, food carts and some restaurants and bars are cash only.

Cell Phones
The US uses CDMA-800 and GSM-1900 bands. SIM cards are relatively easy to obtain.

Time
Pacific Standard Time (GMT minus eight hours)

Tipping
The standard in most circumstances is 15% to 20% of the pretax bill.

Daily Budget

Budget: Less than $150
Dorm bed: $40
Pizza or sandwich: $10
Happy-hour drink and snacks: $20
Light-rail day pass: $5

Midrange: $150–250
Hotel room with queen bed: $180
Nice dinner: $40
Craft cocktail: $13
Museum ticket: $15

Top End: More than $250
Top-end hotel with king bed: $250–350
Prix-fixe dinner: $100–150
Bottle of wine with dinner: $55
Massage at a spa: $95

Advance Planning

Three months before Make reservations at top restaurants; book hotel accommodations.

One month before Book food tours and classes. Purchase tickets for theater shows; concerts or Trail Blazers games at the Moda Center; or Timbers or Thorns games at Providence Park.

One week before Reserve places on walking tours and distillery or brewery tours.

Arriving in Portland

✈ Portland International Airport

The airport is around 20 to 40 minutes from downtown Portland.

Light Rail

The MAX runs from the airport to downtown (adult/child $2.50/1.25).

Taxi & Rideshare

Around $35 to $40 to downtown.

🚉 Union Station

Amtrak trains arrive in the city center.

🚉 Greyhound Depot

Coaches arrive here next to Union Station. Bus and light-rail stop outside.

Getting Around

🚲 Bicycle

Biketown (www.biketownpdx.com) is the city bike-share program; several shops rent bikes.

🚌 Bus

Trimet Bus has routes that connect downtown with outer neighborhoods (adult/child $2.50/1.25).

🚗 Taxi & Rideshare

Must be called in advance. Rideshare services are plentiful.

🚉 Light Rail

The MAX runs all over the city. Trains depart every 15 minutes (adult/child $2.50/1.25).

🚉 Streetcar

Lines connect downtown with the eastern and northwestern districts (adult/child $2/1).

Portland Neighborhoods

Northwest & the Pearl District (p67)
Hip high-rises of the Pearl District give way to fancy Victorian homes around Nob Hill, in this moneyed mélange of top-notch shopping, restaurants and parks.

Northeast (p83)
Ethnically diverse but gentrifying at light speed, Northeast brings together hippies, hipsters, innovative newcomers and long-time resident families in a wide variety of neighborhoods.

Downtown (p29)
Tall buildings, business suits, eclectic food-cart pods, people-filled Pioneer Courthouse Square and the best museums in town make this the bustling center of Portland.

Old Town Chinatown (p51)
Head through Chinese arches to this evolving, gritty part of town filled with urban street-inspired shops and restaurants, and hot nightlife.

Southeast (p101)
Thanks to its relative affordability, this creative-filled quadrant is a nucleus for everything Portland is famous for: food carts, beer, cocktails, coffee and freakiness.

Forest Park

Powell's City of Books

Lan Su Chinese Garden

Saturday Market

Tom McCall Waterfront Park

Washington Park

Pioneer Courthouse Square

Explore
Portland

*Scattered across five quadrants (with a sixth in the works)
Portland's neighborhoods are unique microcosms of
hyperlocal culture. It's almost as if the city is made up of
tons of small towns that got stapled together – each has a
distinct sense of community and special character.*

Explore ⊕
Downtown

The workaday Southwest section of Portland is home to some top sights. It's also a transit hub and where you'll find the city's biggest food-cart pods. Several green parks, important performing-arts centers and plenty of top-end restaurants keep it even more lively.

The Short List

o **Pioneer Courthouse Square (p32)** People-watching, admiring sculptures and gathering for events in Portland's 'living room.'

o **Tom McCall Waterfront Park (p30)** Strolling an expanse of cherry-tree-lined paths, taking in monuments or checking out a festival along the Willamette River.

o **Cultural District institutions (p40)** Taking in art exhibitions, historic displays and performances at the city's top cultural institutions.

o **Restaurants and lounges (p42)** Enjoying creations made with local ingredients by some of Portland's award-winning chefs.

Getting There & Around

🚆 All MAX Light Rail lines (Blue, Green, Red, Yellow and Orange) run through downtown.

🚋 All streetcar lines (NS, A Loop, B Loop) run through downtown.

🚌 Most routes serve downtown; key routes include 4, 9, 14, 15, 19, 20 and 63.

Neighborhood Map on p38

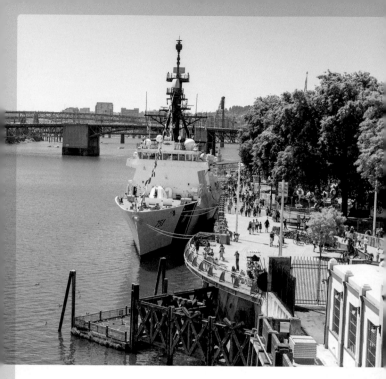

Top Experience 📷

Stroll by the River at Tom McCall Waterfront Park

This 1.5-mile-long park stretches along the banks of the Willamette River and is home to many of the city's events and festivals. Within the park are several historical sights, and its expansive paths – lined with cherry trees that explode with blossoms in springtime – are popular for strolling and cycling.

◎ MAP P38, F5

Naito Pkwy

🚈 Red, Blue

🚌 12, 15, 35

This popular riverside park was finished in 1978 after four years of construction. It replaced an old freeway with paved sidewalks and grassy spaces, and now attracts joggers, in-line skaters, strollers and cyclists.

What's Happening on the Waterfront

The season kicks off with the **Rose Festival** (www.rosefestival.org; ⊙late May–mid-Jun), followed by Portland's **LGBTIQ+ Pride Festival** (www.pridenw.org; ⊙mid-Jun), one of the largest in the Pacific Northwest.

Throughout July, beer and music festivals occupy the park, such as the **Oregon Brewers Festival** (www.oregonbrewfest.com; admission free, 10-token tasting package $20, additional tokens $1) and the **Waterfront Blues Festival** (www.waterfrontbluesfest.com; 4-day passes from $50).

Just north of the Bill Naito Legacy Fountain, an open-sided pavilion shelters the Saturday Market (p54) on weekends from March to December.

Cherry Trees

The Japanese American Historical Plaza (p60), just north of the Burnside Bridge, is linked by one hundred ornamental cherry trees northward to the **Friendship Circle**, a collaborative monument by sculptor Lee Kelly and composer Michael Stirling just west of the Steel Bridge.

Tom McCall

Named after former Oregon governor Tom McCall – a staunch advocate for environmental preservation and proponent for green urban planning – the land that currently forms the park was once the site of Portland's rollicking port. It was also home to the Portland Public Market from 1933 to 1942 and the Harbor Drive Freeway went through here from the 1940s to the 1970s. The park was completed in 1978 and named after McCall (who called for its development) in 1984.

★ Top Tips

o Get a great view of Portland's bridges from here, especially the Hawthorne, Morrison, Burnside and Steel Bridges.

o With its proximity to downtown office buildings, the park's peak hours are around lunchtime, between 11am and 1pm. The paths also see a lot of commuter bike traffic from 3pm to 5pm.

✕ Take a Break

The park's lawns were practically made for picnics – pack your own or pick up something to go from Pine Street Market (p62).

For a meaty meal with a waterfront view, check out LeChon (p62), located towards the northern end of the park.

Downtown Stroll by the River at Tom McCall Waterfront Park

Top Experience
Explore Pioneer Courthouse Square

Affectionately referred to as Portland's 'living room,' Pioneer Courthouse Square is a nucleus of activity for the city. It is the most visited site in Portland and has hosted countless civic and community-driven events since its opening in April 1984. Home to everything from beer festivals to political protests, it draws some 26,000 people to its brick-laden steps each day.

◉ MAP P38, D4

www.thesquarepdx.org

🚇 Red, Blue, Green

The Weather Machine

One of Pioneer Courthouse Square's quirkiest sights is its 'Weather Machine', a 33ft-tall metal column crowned with a large silver orb that reveals the weather forecast for the following day.

The orb opens up to reveal one of three metal icons: a gold-leaf sun to represent a clear day; a silver great blue heron to indicate a drizzly or overcast day; and an open-mouthed copper dragon that forecasts stormy, windy days with heavy rainfall.

Finally, reminiscent of a mercury thermometer, a vertical display of light bulbs illuminate to show the temperature in 10-degree increments. An additional light system below the orb indicates air quality: green for good, amber for slight smog, and red for suboptimal conditions.

Events

Pioneer Courthouse Square hosts more than 300 functions each year. Its two brick amphitheaters provide seating for musical performances and events like Flicks on the Bricks (p46), a free summer outdoor movie series that takes place on Friday nights. Other recurring summer events include 'Meditation Mondays', a 30-minute guided group meditation; 'Noon Tunes' on Tuesdays, a series of weekly, hour-long free concerts; and 'Wellness Wednesdays', featuring an hour of free activities such as yoga, tai chi, Zumba and Pilates.

During the holiday season, a tall Christmas tree occupies the square's center, with its lighting ceremony taking place each year on the Friday after Thanksgiving. There's also a 'Tuba Christmas' event, which features 200 to 300 tuba and euphonium players performing holiday songs.The square is also home to the annual **Holiday Ale Festival** (www.holidayale.com; tickets $40; ☾early Dec).

★ Top Tips

o Check the live broadcast of the square (www.kgw.com/pioneer-square) to get a sense of the crowds during any major events.

o During non-event times, the scene at the square may appear underwhelming – but it's a great place to take a break when downtown.

o The Travel Portland (p152) visitor center at the square has a high-tech, all-gender, ADA-accessible restroom.

✗ Take a Break

If you need a quick pick-me-up, head one block northwest to Public Domain Coffee (p46).

For something stronger, the chic Departure Lounge (p45) is two blocks east and offers fantastic rooftop views.

Not all of the square's events are cheery in nature – it's also a key venue for many of the city's political demonstrations, rallies, vigils and speeches.

Visit the Pioneer Courthouse Square website for an events calendar.

History

Named after the adjacent Pioneer Courthouse, the Pacific Northwest's oldest federal building, the square got its beginnings in 1849 when shoemaker Elijah Hill acquired the land for $24 and a pair of boots. The local school board then purchased the block in 1858, opening Portland's first public school, the Central School. In 1890 the school was moved and the land became the site of the eight-story Portland Hotel – the archway and gate-work of which are still part of the square today.

The hotel was razed in 1951 to make way for a two-story parking garage, and in the late 1960s, developers proposed an even larger 12-story parking structure in its place. The city denied this plan, and between 1972 and 1974, they purchased the block, settled on its future as a public-use space, and instituted an international competition for its design.

In 1980 a Portland-based architect Willard Martin and his design team won the competition, beating 160 contestants with their plans for a multiuse urban plaza. But funding problems soon surfaced – construction of the square required over

Pioneer Courthouse Square

The Man with the Umbrella & More

Standing 6ft 10in and weighing 460lb, the **Allow Me** sculpture depicts a man in a business suit, holding an umbrella and hailing a cab. One of seven casts by artist John Seward Johnson II, the sculpture was donated for the square in 1984.

There are several other bronze sculptures throughout the square including five bronze masks designed by Willard Martin, the architect who designed the square (find them in the water trough next to Starbucks). And in tribute to Martin, there is a bronze replica of his top hat next to the top of the fountain, above the visitor center.

The northwestern corner of the square features an **Echo Chamber** – stand on the round marble stone in the center of the small amphitheater, face the steps, and speak out loud to hear a reverberating echo of your own voice for a startlingly fun auditory experience.

$7 million for land acquisition, structures and amenities.

City commissioners formed the 'Friends of Pioneer Square' citizens' group and raised over $1.5 million by selling bricks inscribed with donors' names (you can still buy one for $100), which would be supplemented by other donations and grant funding, plus a matching of dollars through federal funding. Four years later, on 6 April 1984, Pioneer Courthouse Square officially opened with a celebration that drew more than 10,000 attendees.

Designed for Living

At first glance, Pioneer Courthouse Square may appear merely as a plaza comprised of red bricks – but take a closer look and you'll notice architectural intricacies that reveal a rich artistic and historical significance for the city of Portland.

Framing the entrance of the visitor center is the **Waterfall fountain**, where water cascades down granite steps into twin pools. At the top of the fountain is a 'Keystone Lectern', which was designed to be a focal speaking platform and serves as a good vantage point for overlooking the activities of the square.

The square occupies a full, 40,000-sq-ft city block. Its center is laid out like an amphitheater, with two dozen steps arranged in a semicircle functioning as seats during performances or events. Surrounding the square is a set of towering classical pillars that progressively 'topple' in the style of ancient ruins. The tops of the pillars feature carvings of yellow roses with pink- and green-spotted insects, and some 'fallen' ones are topped with bronze chess boards.

Walking Tour 🥾

Downtown Stroll

Stroll the heart of Portland from Pioneer Courthouse Square, the city's 'living room,' to museums, Portland State University, open markets, fountains and of course the banks of the lovely Willamette River. Along the way pay homage to the Goddess of Commerce and the city's Japanese heritage.

Walk Facts

Start Pioneer Courthouse Square (🚊 Red, Blue, Green)

End Japanese American Historical Plaza (🚊 Red, Blue)

Length 2.2 miles; 1½ hours

❶ Weather Machine

Begin your exploration at **Pioneer Courthouse Square** (p32), and get a forecast from the square's 33ft-tall 'Weather Machine' beacon at noon everyday.

❷ Trees, art & history

From there, head two blocks south along Broadway, then pop over a block on SW Salmon St to the **South Park Blocks** (p40), a 12-block-long greenway. Stroll along the leafy paths, with eyes out for the **Portland Art Museum** (p41) and the **Oregon Historical Society** (p40) on either side of the esplanade.

❸ Shop the University

If you catch yourself in the area on a Saturday, the farmers market at **Portland State University** (p40) is worth walking south to SW Montgomery St. Here, more than 100 vendors sell produce and freshly prepared goodies, and you'll also find a variety of food carts.

❹ Portlandia

From there, make your way northeast to the **Portland Building** (p40) on SW 5th Ave between SW Madison and SW Main Sts. It's worth passing for a glimpse of **Portlandia**, a 34ft bronze statute of Portland's supposed patroness, the Goddess of Commerce – it's the second-largest hammered-copper statue in the country after the Statue of Liberty.

❺ Waterfront parks

Head a block north to SW Salmon St and turn right to continue to **Tom McCall Waterfront Park** (p30). Stop at the interactive **Salmon Street Springs Fountain** (p40), which jets water to the beat of computer-generated patterns. A block north is **Mill Ends Park** (p41) – the smallest public park in the world, and the supposed home of leprechauns.

❻ Battleship Oregon

Cross back into Tom McCall park and continue north along the paved waterfront path. Pass the Morrison Bridge to reach the **Battleship Oregon Memorial** – the time capsule inscription at the base of the monument was sealed in 1976 and will be opened in 2076.

❼ To Market

If it's a weekend, you'll be lured near the Burnside Bridge to the **Saturday Market** (p54), where hundreds of local vendors sell everything from art and kitschy souvenirs to clothing and hand-made accessories.

❽ Japanese American Art

North of the Burnside Bridge is the **Japanese American Historical Plaza** (p60), which features art dedicated to the Pacific Northwest's Japanese immigrants and native US citizens of Japanese descent who were sent to intern-ment camps during WWII. Cherry trees lead you north to the **Friend-ship Circle**, an interactive monu-ment playing Japanese music.

Downtown

SW Front Ave (Naito Pkwy)

4

MAX Light Rail

NW 2nd Ave

F

NW 3rd Ave

25 ✪

SW Ankeny St

SW Ash St

13 ✕

SW Pine St

SW Oak St

Oak/SW 1st

3

SW Harvey Milk St

SW Washington St

SW 3rd

SW Oak St

SW Alder St

E NW Couch St

NW Couch St

OLD TOWN CHINATOWN

NW 4th Ave

SW Oak

SW Pine

17 ✕

NW 6th Ave

NW Broadway

SW Pine

SW Ankeny St

Mall SW 5th

Mall SW 4th

2

Pioneer Courthouse

29

SW 6th Ave

21

Pioneer Courthouse

7

Pioneer Place

D

North Park Blocks

NW 8th Ave

NW Park Ave

SW Oak St

SW Harvey Milk St

SW Washington St

SW Alder St

12 ✕ ✕ 15

Pioneer Square N

23

Pioneer Courthouse Square

Pioneer Square S

SW Taylor St

C

NW 9th Ave

20 ⊕

NW 10th Ave

28

22 ✕

SW Park Ave

19

SW 9th Ave

Pioneer Square N

Travel Portland

TriMet Information Center

Pioneer Courthouse Square

1

NW 11th Ave

14 ✕

SW 10th Ave

Galleria SW 10th

Library SW 9th

SW Morrison St

SW Yamhill St

SW Taylor St

SW Salmon St

NW 12th Ave

11 ✕

SW 11th Ave

SW 12th Ave

B

18 ✕

NW 13th Ave

MAX Light Rail

SW 13th Ave

SW Main St

NW 14th Ave

26 ✪

SW 14th Ave

W Burnside St

A

1

2

3

4

Downtown

Tom McCall Waterfront Park

Yamhill District

Portland Spirit 9

Mill Ends Park

Willamette River

Hawthorne Bridge

8

SW 1st Ave

SW 2nd Ave

10

SW 3rd Ave

SW 4th Ave

SW 5th Ave

Salmon Street Springs Fountain

1

200 m
0.1 miles

SW Madison St

SW Jefferson St

SW Columbia St

SW Clay St

SW Market St

SW 1st Ave

SW Clay St 24

SW Market St

SW 3rd Ave

SW 4th Ave

Pettygrove Park

Lownsdale Sq

Chapman Sq

Portland Building 4

City Hall

SW Jefferson

DOWNTOWN

SW Salmon St

SW Main St

SW Madison St

SW Madison

27

16

SW Jefferson St

SW Columbia St

SW Clay St

SW Market St

SW Broadway

SW Mill St

SW Mill

SW Montgomery St

SW Montgomery

SW Harrison St

Oregon Historical Society

5

Portland Art Museum 6

South Park Blocks

SW Park Ave

South Park Blocks 3

SW 10th Ave

Portland State University 2

SW 12th Ave

Portland Streetcar

SW Harrison St

SW Hall St

Sights

Salmon Street Springs Fountain
FOUNTAIN

1 ◉ MAP P38, F6

This photo-friendly fountain, on Salmon St near the river, cycles through computer-generated patterns. On hot days kids (and adults) take turns plunging through the jets. (1000 SW Naito Pkwy; 🚍4, 10, 14, 15, 30)

Portland State University
LANDMARK

2 ◉ MAP P38, A7

This pretty campus is at the southwestern corner of downtown. There's a good farmers market here on Saturday, and several food carts around. (1825 SW Broadway)

South Park Blocks
PARK

3 ◉ MAP P38, B7

The South Park Blocks, a 12-block-long greenway that runs through much of downtown, are a fine, leafy refuge from downtown's bustle. They host a farmers market, occasional art shows, and are home to the Oregon Historical Society museum and the excellent Portland Art Museum. At the southern end of the South Park Blocks is Portland State University.

Portland Building
LANDMARK

4 ◉ MAP P38, D5

This controversial 15-story building (1982) was designed by Michael Graves and catapulted the postmodern architect to celebrity status. But the blocky edifice has never been popular with the people who work inside it. In addition, the city found structural problems that led to massive reconstruction works, which were completed in 2020.

Crouched over the main doors of the Portland Building is **Portlandia**. Made by sculptor Raymond Kaskey, the figure is, at just over 34ft, the second-largest hammered-copper statue in the US (after the Statue of Liberty). (1120 SW 5th Ave)

Oregon Historical Society
MUSEUM

5 ◉ MAP P38, B5

Along the tree-shaded South Park Blocks sits the state's primary history museum, which in 2019 unveiled a permanent 7000-sq-ft interactive exhibit that delves into Oregon's history, peoples and landscape. Stations include a canoe-building exercise, a walk-through covered-wagon replica and historical role-playing games. There are interesting sections on various immigrant groups, Native American tribes and the travails of the Oregon Trail. Temporary exhibits furnish the downstairs space. Check the website for free admission days. (📞503-222-1741; www.ohs.org; 1200 SW Park Ave; adult/child $10/5; ⏰10am-5pm Mon-Sat, noon-5pm Sun; 🚊Red, Blue)

Portland Art Museum   MUSEUM

6 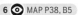 MAP P38, B5

Portland Art Museum's excellent exhibits include Native American carvings, Asian and American art, photography and English silver. The museum also houses the Whitsell Auditorium, a first-rate theater that frequently screens rare or international films and that is part of the Northwest Film Center and school. (☎503-226-2811; www. portlandartmuseum.org; 1219 SW Park Ave; adult/child $20/free; ☺10am-5pm Tue, Wed, Sat & Sun, to 8pm Thu & Fri; 🚍6, 38, 45, 55, 58, 68, 92, 96, 🚋NS Line, A-Loop)

Pioneer Courthouse   HISTORIC BUILDING

7 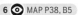 MAP P38, D4

Across 6th Ave from Pioneer Courthouse Square is the Pioneer Courthouse. Built in 1875, this was the legal center of 19th-century Portland. The courthouse's public areas, including the cupola, with views over downtown, are open to visitors. (www.pioneercourthouse. org; 700 SW 6th Ave; admission free; ☺public areas 9am-4pm Mon-Fri; 🚋Red, Blue, Green)

Mill Ends Park   PARK

8 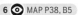 MAP P38, F5

Having the largest park (Forest Park) within city limits perhaps isn't an oddity, but having the

Salmon Street Springs Fountain

GAGLIARDIPHOTOGRAPHY/SHUTTERSTOCK ©

Local Experiences

Hangouts For a breather between bouts of sightseeing and shopping, head to Pioneer Courthouse Square (p32). Grab a bite from one of the food carts here and settle onto the brick steps for grade-A people-watching, or bring a chess set and have a game.

Happy-hour grub There's no need to wait for dinner to experience some of Portland's best dining – most restaurants open up for happy hour before dinner service starts, and offer comprehensive menus that allow you to try house specialties in smaller portions for a fraction of the price.

Farmers-market food carts Development has resulted in the demise of the downtown's biggest food-cart pod, but you'll still find a few scattered throughout. Portland State University (p40) is home to a wonderful farmers market on Saturday, which has plenty of on-site food carts.

First Thursday Art Walk (www.firstthursdayportland.com) On the first Thursday of each month, many galleries extend their evening hours and show off new exhibits, often with wine and snacks. It's a bit of a mob scene but it's fun and fascinating.

smallest one might be. Mill Ends Park – located on a median strip – is a circle of green 24in in diameter (it's the reputed home of leprechauns). (SW Naito Pkwy & Taylor St)

Portland Spirit CRUISE

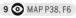 9 MAP P38, F6

Tour Portland from the water: these cruises offer sightseeing, historical narratives and/or meal combinations. (☑503-224-3900; www.portlandspirit.com; sightseeing/dinner cruise from $32/78; ☐4, 10, 14, 15, 30)

Eating

Luc Lac VIETNAMESE $

10 MAP P38, E5

This bustling Vietnamese kitchen draws downtown lunch crowds and late-night bar-hoppers with superbly executed classics like pho, vermicelli bowls and bahn mi. Count on queueing any time of day to score a seat in the swanky dining room, where pink paper parasols hang from the ceiling. Happy hour (4pm to 7pm) has a more relaxed vibe and small plates run just $3. (☑503-222-0047; www.luclackitchen.com; 835 SW 2nd Ave; mains $9-13; ⊙11am-2:30pm & 4pm-midnight Sun-Thu, 11am-2:30pm & 4pm-4am Fri & Sat)

Bullard SOUTHERN US $$

Inside the Woodlark hotel (see 19 Map p38, C3) is this nod to chef Doug Adam's roots and chosen home, where the meat-centric menu is decidedly Texas-meets-Oregon. 'Supper' plates showcase the likes of 12-hour smoked Painted Hills beef ribs served with fresh flour tortillas, grilled rainbow trout with a black-eyed pea and celery salad, and a pork chop with heirloom hominy and local collard greens. (☎503-222-1670; www.bullardpdx.com; 813 SW Alder St; dinner mains $16-32; ⏱11am-3pm & 5-10pm Mon-Thu, 11am-3pm & 5-11pm Fri, 10am-11pm Sat, 10am-10pm Sun)

Tasty n Alder FUSION $$

11 ✖ MAP P38, B2

Another of local restaurateur John Gorham's empire of Portland eateries, this downtown corner joint serves locally sourced, American interpretations of international dishes – duck breast grilled on a Spanish *plancha* or the awesome Korean *bibimbap* (rice, veggies and chili paste) served with bacon and eggs. Go for brunch on a weekday to avoid the crowds. (☎503-621-9251; www.tastynalder.com; 580 SW 12th Ave; mains $12-35; ⏱9am-2pm & 5:30-10pm Sun-Thu, to 11pm Fri & Sat; 🚌15, 51)

The Crown PIZZA $$

12 ✖ MAP P38, D2

Sister restaurant to chef Vitaly Paley's Imperial, this New York–style pizza joint inside Hotel Lucia is both a perfect lunch spot and a killer cocktail bar. Options include the signature Imperial pie, with fried chicken, pickles and ranch dressing, plus snacks, salads and slices. Large groups can go all-out with the 36in-long Al Metro, aka 'big-ass pizza' ($48). (☎503-228-7224; www.thecrownpdx.com; 410 SW Broadway; slices $4.75-6.75, pizzas $15-28; ⏱11:30am-midnight Mon-Fri, from 3pm Sat & Sun)

Mother's Bistro AMERICAN $$

13 ✖ MAP P38, F2

Mother's is an upscale downtown spot beloved for its breakfast – try the salmon hash. For dinner, comfort food dishes include chicken and dumplings and meatloaf with gravy. The bright, cozy dining room features gilded accents and crystal chandeliers for a touch of class. You're guaranteed to wait in line on weekends. (☎503-464-1122; www.mothersbistro.com; 121 SW 3rd Ave; breakfast mains $9-17; ⏱7am-2:30pm & 5:30-9pm Tue-Thu, to 10pm Fri, 8am-2:30pm & 5-10pm Sat, 8am-2:30pm Sun)

Kenny & Zuke's DELI $$

14 ✖ MAP P38, B2

The only place in the city for real Jewish deli food: bagels, pickled herring, homemade pickles and latkes (potato pancakes). But the real draw is the house pastrami, cut to order and gently sandwiched in one of the best Reubens you'll ever eat. It bustles for breakfast, too. (☎503-222-3354; www.kennyandzukes.com; 1038 SW Harvey Milk St; sandwiches $10-20; ⏱7am-8pm Mon-Thu, to 9pm Fri, 8am-9pm Sat, 8am-8pm Sun)

Imperial

AMERICAN $$$

15 MAP P38, D2

Opened by long-adored Portland chef Vitaly Paley, the Imperial – attached to Hotel Lucia (www.hotellucia.com) – is huge in scale but fastidious and detail-oriented in approach. The kitchen is built around a massive wood-fire grill and rotisserie, and the menu exploits seasonal Northwest bounty – from rib eye and roasted chicken to grilled asparagus and ember-roasted potatoes. Great happy hour, too. (503-228-7222; www.imperialpdx.com; 410 SW Broadway; mains $11-45; 6:30am-10pm Mon-Thu, to 11pm Fri, 8am-11pm Sat, to 10pm Sun)

Higgins

FRENCH, NORTHWESTERN $$$

16 MAP P38, C6

In 1994 chef-owner Greg Higgins opened the doors to one of Portland's groundbreaking restaurants. These days, Higgins feels more classically elegant than cutting edge, but it still features French-inspired dishes like duck confit with brandied cherries, using seasonal Northwest ingredients. The beer list is among the best in town; ask for pairing suggestions for any course. (503-222-9070; www.higginsportland.com; 1239 SW Broadway; mains $26-47; 11:30am-midnight Mon-Fri, from 5pm Sat & Sun)

Little Bird

FRENCH $$$

17 MAP P38, D2

Sister restaurant to lower E Burnside's renowned Le Pigeon (p111) is this quaint French bistro. Folks swoon over the *poulet et porc* and chicken-fried trout; don't miss the pricey but sublime desserts ($11 to $15). It also serves a double-brie burger with spiced ketchup, one of Portland's best ($16). (503-688-5952; www.littlebirdbistro.com; 215 SW 6th Ave; mains $16-39; 11:30am-11pm Mon-Fri, from 5pm Sat & Sun)

Jake's Famous Crawfish

SEAFOOD $$$

18 MAP P38, B2

Saunter into this classic joint, reservation in hand. You'll need it – some of Portland's best seafood can be found here within an elegant old-time atmosphere. The oysters are divine, the crab cakes a revelation and the seafood-stuffed Chinook salmon your ticket to heaven. Come at happy hour for more affordable treats. (503-226-1419; www.jakesfamouscrawfish.com; 401 SW 12th Ave; mains $22-47; 11:30am-10pm Mon-Thu, to 11pm Fri & Sat, 10am-10pm Sun)

Drinking

Abigail Hall

COCKTAIL BAR

19 MAP P38, C3

Just beyond the lobby of the Woodlark hotel (https://

MARK YOUSO/SHUTTERSTOCK ©

Jake's Famous Crawfish

woodlarkhotel.com) is Abigail Hall, the hotel bar named after an Oregon suffragette and the women's reception hall that once inhabited the historic space. Retro floral wallpaper, stiff-backed banquettes and plaid wingback chairs deliver a punch of granny chic, while cocktails with names like 'Born on the Bayeux' and 'Summer in Aberdeen' conjure foregone times.

There's a good bar menu that includes prawn cocktails, fried chicken fingers, steak bites and a Dungeness crab roll. (www.abigailhallpdx.com; 813 SW Alder St; ⏰3pm-late)

Courier Coffee Roasters

COFFEE

20 MAP P38, C1

Courier is a small-batch roaster with friendly baristas and a great macchiato. Exceptional pastries, too. Go for an iced drink on a hot day. It delivers its roasted beans by cargo bicycle, among other sustainable practices. (☎503-545-6444; www.couriercoffeeroasters.com; 923 SW Oak St; ⏰7am-6pm Mon-Fri, 9am-5pm Sat & Sun; 📶)

Departure Lounge

BAR

21 MAP P38, D4

This rooftop restaurant-bar, atop the 15th floor of the Nines hotel (www.thenines.com), fills a deep downtown void: a cool bar with

© FOXFOTO/SHUTTERSTOCK ©

Crystal Ballroom

unforgettable views of Portland. The vibe is distinctly 'spaceship LA,' with mod couches and sleek lighting. Hit happy hour from 4pm to 6pm (or late night) for select drinks and appetizers. (☏503-802-5370; www.departureportland.com; 525 SW Morrison St; ⏰4-11pm Sun-Thu, to midnight Fri & Sat; 🚋1, 8, 12, 94, 🚊Green, Yellow, Blue, Red)

Public Domain Coffee

COFFEE

22 ☕ MAP P38, C3

A swanky downtown outlet with shiny high-end espresso machines, owned by long-time indie roasters Coffee Bean International. (☏503-243-6374; www.publicdomaincoffee.com; 603 SW Broadway; ⏰6am-5pm; 📶)

Entertainment

Flicks on the Bricks

CINEMA

23 ⭐ MAP P38, D4

On certain Fridays in summer, the Pioneer Courthouse Square becomes a huge outdoor cinema showing free movies on a big screen. Bring your own chairs or take a seat on the brick steps. (www.thesquarepdx.org/events; ⏰7pm Fri Jul & Aug; 🚊Red, Blue Green)

Keller Auditorium

PERFORMING ARTS

24 ⭐ MAP P38, D7

Built in 1917 and formerly known as the Civic Auditorium, Keller hosts a wide range of performers, from big-name musicians (Sturgill Simpson) to the Portland Opera (www.portlandopera.org) and the Oregon Ballet Theatre (www.obt.org), along with some Broadway productions. (☏503-248-4335; www.portland5.com; 222 SW Clay St; 🚋38, 45, 55, 92, 96)

Dante's

LIVE MUSIC

25 ⭐ MAP P38, F1

This steamy red bar books burlesque and cabaret shows along with national and regional touring bands (including the Murder City Devils, the Supersuckers and the Sugarhill Gang). Drop in on Sunday night for the eclectic Sinferno Cabaret, and on Monday night for Karaoke from Hell. (☏tickets

866-777-8932; www.danteslive.com;
350 W Burnside St)

Crystal Ballroom
LIVE MUSIC

26 ⭐ MAP P38, A1

This large, historic ballroom has
hosted some major acts, including
James Brown and Marvin Gaye
in the early '60s, and Devendra
Banhart and Two Door Cinema
Club today. The bouncy, 'floating'
dance floor makes dancing almost
effortless. (📞503-225-0047; www.
crystalballroompdx.com; 1332 W Burnside St; 🚍20)

Arlene Schnitzer Concert Hall
CLASSICAL MUSIC

27 ⭐ MAP P38, C5

This beautiful, if not acoustically
brilliant, downtown venue, built
in 1928, hosts a wide range of
shows, lectures, concerts and
other performances. (📞503-248-
4335; www.portland5.com; 1037 SW
Broadway; 🚍10, 14, 15, 35, 36, 44,
54, 56)

Shopping

Tender Loving Empire
GIFTS & SOUVENIRS

28 🔒 MAP P38, C2

This small gift shop is so Portland it
hurts: in addition to selling adorable
handmade goods by local 'makers,'

Big Brands, No Sales Tax

The downtown area is
where you'll find a majority
of Portland's outposts for
big-name brands, primarily
around Pioneer Place Mall
and near Pioneer Courthouse
Square. There are lots of local
boutiques and concept stores
in the area as well, particularly
northwest of Pioneer Courthouse Square, running up to W
Burnside St. And remember,
there's no sales tax in Oregon
so everything is likely cheaper
than you'll find at home.

it's also an independent record
label, with in-store listening station,
plus a tiny art gallery. Can you
guess it's really into promoting local
art and creativity? (📞503-243-5859;
www.tenderlovingempire.com; 412 SW
10th Ave; 🕙10:30am-6:30pm)

Pioneer Place
MALL

29 🔒 MAP P38, D4

A big, semi-upscale shopping
center downtown, Pioneer Place
has a food court in the basement
and is handy to public transit.
(📞503-228-5800; www.pioneerplace.
com; 700 SW 5th Ave; 🕙10am-8pm
Mon-Sat, 11am-6pm Sun)

Top Experience 📷
Enjoy the greenery at Washington Park

Tame and well-tended Washington Park contains several attractions within its 410 green acres. The International Rose Test Garden is the centerpiece of Portland's famous rose blooms. Further uphill is the Japanese Garden, another oasis of tranquility. If you have kids, the Oregon Zoo and Portland Children's Museum should be on your docket.

www.washington
parkpdx.org

👫

🚌 63, 🚊 Blue, Red
🚊 Washington Park

Gardens Galore

Often called the most authentic Japanese garden outside Japan, the **Japanese Garden** (☎503-223-1321; www.japanesegarden.org; 611 SW Kingston Ave; adult/child $17/11.50; ⏰noon-7pm Mon, 10am-7pm Tue-Sun mid-Mar–Sep, to 4pm Oct–mid-Mar) is a sanctuary. It was conceived as a symbol of post-WWII healing between the US and Japan when Portland and Sapporo became sister cities in 1959.

Meanwhile, the **International Rose Test Garden** (pictured; www.waparkrosefriends.org; 400 SW Kingston Ave; admission free; ⏰7:30am-9pm) practically gave Portland its 'Rose City' nickname. It sprawls across 4.5 acres of lawns, fountains and flowerbeds, and on a clear day you can catch peeks of downtown and Mt Hood. Over 700 rose varieties grow here; from April to September the scent is intoxicating.

Hoyt Arboretum

Twelve miles of trails wind through this 189-acre ridge-top **garden** (☎503-865-8733; www.hoytarboretum.org; 4000 Fairview Blvd; admission free; ⏰trails 5am-10pm, visitor center 9am-4pm Mon-Fri, from 10am Sat & Sun) above the city zoo. It's home to over 6000 native and exotic plants and trees representing 1100 different species, and it offers easy walks any time of year.

Washington Park for Kids

The well-run **Oregon Zoo** (☎503-226-1561; www.oregonzoo.org; 4001 SW Canyon Rd; adult/child $18/13; ⏰9:30am-6pm Jun-Aug, to 4pm Sep-May; 👪) has many impressive exhibits. Enclosures are spacious and semi-natural. Concerts take place on the zoo's lawns in summer.

On rainy days, families can seek solace at the **Portland Children's Museum** (☎503-233-6500; www.portlandcm.org; 4015 SW Canyon Rd; $11, 2nd Sunday of each month 9am-noon $3; ⏰9am-5pm; 👪), a great place to keep kids busy with interesting learning activities and exhibits.

★ **Top Tips**

● Complimentary Japanese Garden tours typically take place at 2pm and 4pm from May 1 through Labor Day, and at noon from September 4 through April 30. Call to confirm.

● From June to late September, volunteers lead Rose Garden tours daily, starting from the Rose Garden Store at 1pm (call ahead to confirm).

✗ **Take a Break**

The Japanese Garden's **Umami Cafe** serves traditional Japanese tea sets served with sweets or savory dishes like fried rice bowls.

★ **Getting There**

Light Rail Red and Blue lines.

Bus Routes 15 and 20.

Shuttle The Explore Washington Park Shuttle runs May to October and stops at the park's major attractions.

Explore ⊕
Old Town
Chinatown

The core of rambunctious 1890s Portland, once-seedy Old Town was the lurking ground of unsavory characters. Now it's home to historic buildings, Waterfront Park, the Saturday Market and good nightlife.

Old Town is generally lumped together with historic Chinatown – no longer the heart of the Chinese community, but home to the ornate Chinatown Gateway and the Lan Su Chinese Garden.

The Short List

o **Lan Su Chinese Garden (p52)** Admiring the traditional architecture and landscaped haven.

o **Saturday Market (p54)** Browsing creations in the country's largest and longest-running open-art arts-and-crafts market.

o **Japanese American Historical Plaza (p60)** Reflecting on the Pacific Northwest's Japanese-American residents who were forced into internment camps during WWII.

o **Darcelle XV (p64)** Reveling in the big-wig, cabaret splendor, all led by the city's octogenarian drag queen.

o **Voodoo Doughnut (p61)** Queuing for creative doughnuts – and taking them to go in a big pink box.

Getting There & Around

🚊 The Red and Blue MAX light-rail lines run along 1st Ave on the eastern side of the district; the Yellow and Green lines run along NW 6th Ave on the western side.

🚌 Routes 1, 4, 5, 8, 10, 16, 33, 40 and 77 serve the area.

Neighborhood Map on p58

Lan Su Chinese Garden (p52) ARTYOORAN/SHUTTERSTOCK ©

Top Experience 📷

Relax at Tranquil Lan Su Chinese Garden

A tranquil oasis set in the bustle of the city, Lan Su Chinese Garden is a wonderful place to reflect among nature and learn about Chinese culture. Spanning 40,000 sq ft, the authentic Ming Dynasty–style space features koi ponds, seasonal foliage and traditional architecture. Cultural events and demonstrations by community organizations and local experts take place year-round.

◎ MAP P58, C2

📞 503-228-8131

www.lansugarden.org

239 NW Everett St

adult/student $11/8

🕙 10am-7pm mid-May–mid-Oct, shorter hours rest of year

🚌 8, 77, 🚆 Blue, Red

Architecture & Landscape

As one of the most traditional Chinese gardens in the US, Lan Su's grounds feature pavilions, bridges, open colonnades, covered walkways, ponds and meticulously tended foliage.

In 1988 Suzhou, China, was designated a sister city of Portland, fueling ambitions for creating a traditional Chinese garden in the city. More than a decade later, in 1999, 65 artisans from Suzhou began constructing the walled botanical complex on a plot of land donated by the Northwest Natural Gas Company.

Native Chinese flora that shifts with the seasons is found throughout the garden's verdant landscape. Horticulture enthusiasts can learn more about Lan Su's landscape during the 45-minute 'plant walk' guided tour that takes place every Tuesday at 2pm.

Art

In the garden pavilions, Lan Su showcases classic and contemporary works by artists from the Pacific Northwest and beyond. Visitors can also partake in a range of demonstrations on calligraphy, poetry and brush and silk painting from classically trained artists and scholars.

Culture

Everything at Lan Su represents harmony, beauty and a reverence for tradition – even its name, which is a derivation of both Portland ('Lan') and Suzhou ('Su'). 'Lan' is the Chinese word for 'orchid', and 'su' is the word for 'arise' or 'awaken', making Lan Su's poetic appellation 'garden of awakening orchids'.

Lan Su serves as a beacon of Chinese culture and community in Portland. In partnership with more than 50 local organizations, demonstrations, lessons and other educational events take place almost every day and are typically included with the price of admission.

★ **Top Tips**

o Horticulture enthusiasts should check out Lan Su's 'Bloom Guide,' which features the top 16 varieties of flora visible in the garden during each season. Pick up a copy at the admission desk, or download it from the website.

o Public tours begin in the Courtyard of Tranquility a few times per day, and are included with admission. Check the website for exact days and times.

✕ **Take a Break**

The garden has a two-story **teahouse**, located in the Tower of Cosmic Reflections. Traditional tea presentations are offered, along with pastries, snacks, and light dishes like noodle bowls, dumplings, buns and soups.

Top Experience 📷

Find handcrafted souvenirs at Saturday Market

Established in 1974, Portland's Saturday Market is the longest-running open-air craft market in the US. From March through Christmas Eve, hundreds of hometown vendors hawk everything under the sun on Saturdays and Sundays. It's a one-stop shop for picking up handcrafted creations, checking out musical performances and sampling international food-cart fare.

◎ MAP P58, F5

📞 503-222-6072

www.portland
saturdaymarket.com

2 SW Naito Pkwy

🕙 10am-5pm Sat, 11am-4:30pm Sun Mar-Dec

🚌 12, 16, 19, 20

Ⓡ Red, Blue

Market History

Artists Sheri Teasdale and Andrea Scharf founded the market as a mutual benefit corporation that would require vendors to contribute to costs and administration, but keep all the profits earned from selling their wares. They also determined that everything at the market must be handmade by the seller.

Today, more than 750,000 visit each year, generating some $12 million in gross sales annually.

What to Look For

If you can dream it, you can probably find it at this market. With more than 350 local artisans and craftspeople selling their creations here, variety is the word.

Check out the booths run by everyone from woodworkers and jewelry-makers to folks making dried flowers cast in crystal or blown-glass bird feeders.

It's a great place to score gifts around Christmas too. During the final week of the market, the **Festival of the Last Minute** (11am to 5pm Monday to Friday, 10am to 5pm Saturday, 11am to 3:30pm Sunday) is open every day.

Shop to the Beat

While people-watching at the market makes for great entertainment, you'll also catch local musicians playing original music on the 'Main Stage' next to the Bill Naito Legacy Fountain in Tom McCall Waterfront Park. Genres range from acoustic folk and swing to blues and alternative rock. The tempos are kept upbeat and lively, just like the market's atmosphere.

For mini market-goers, there's a 'Kids' Korner' that has activities such as puppet shows and hands-on craft activities, led by different organizations like the Portland's Children Museum.

★ Top Tips

o Each year, a different artist is commissioned to design the cover of the market's annual souvenir booklet, which includes a map. View it online at www.psmsouvenirbooklet.com, or email info@saturdaymarket.org to receive a printed copy in the mail.

o If you make a $25 purchase at the market, you'll receive a free TriMet ticket or up to two hours of parking validation at any of the city's Smart Park garages.

✗ Take a Break

The market's **International Food Court** has everything from Nepalese to Guatemalan. Grab a bite and keep wandering.

If you need to take a load off, Pine Street Market (p62) is a couple of blocks away.

Old Town Chinatown Find handcrafted souvenirs at Saturday Market

Walking Tour 🚶

Wandering Old Town Chinatown

This walk takes you through some of Portland's rich Asian history and influence as well as to some quirky, modern and off-the-tourist radar stops. Along the way you'll get to stroll the banks of the lovely Willamette River, shop, shoot pinball, re-fuel with coffee and eat tacos for a very Portland-y adventure.

Walk Facts

Start New Market Theater (🚇 Blue)

End Lan Su Chinese Garden (🚌 8, 4; 🚇 Blue)

Length 1 mile; three hours

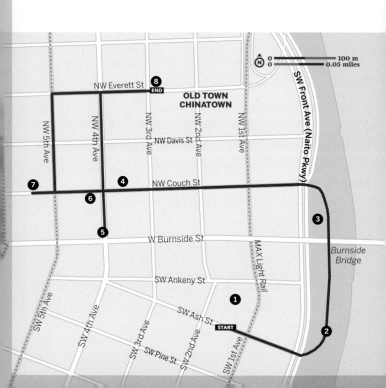

❶ Nostalgic architecture

Kick off your stroll at the **New Market Theater** (p60), where you can admire circa 1872 details such as the arches that face SW 1st Ave. Adding to the nostalgic architecture is the **Skidmore Fountain** (p60), just across the street at the corner of SW 1st Ave and SW Ankeny St.

❷ Market action

If you're here on a weekend, you'll be right in the middle of the **Saturday Market** (p54) action, which spreads all the way to the riverside **Tom McCall Waterfront Park** (p30).

❸ Historic plaza's cherry trees

Located within the park, just north of the Burnside Bridge, is the **Japanese American Historical Plaza** (p60), where one hundred cherry trees line the river.

❹ Handmade goodies

From there, cross over Naito Pkwy to NW Couch St. Continue three blocks to **Kiriko Made** (p64). Browse the handmade clothing and home goods that are all made with vintage Japanese textiles and techniques.

❺ Gateway to Chinatown

Next, walk a block south down NW 4th Ave till you see the **Chinatown Gateway** (p60). After admiring its ornate details, head to **Tope** (p62) on the Hoxton Hotel's rooftop for a drink with a wonderful view.

❻ Caffeine & sneakers & bags, oh my!

Head back up NW 4th Ave and take a left on Couch St. Pop into **Deadstock Coffee** (p63), a laid-back shop dedicated to sneaker culture. Next door, you can watch beautiful leather bags and accessories come to life at family-run **Orox Leather Goods** (p64) – and shop their wares.

❼ Old-skool video games

Continue another block west on Couch St to NW 5th Ave and check out **Ground Kontrol Classic Arcade** (p62) for a round of pinball or old-school video games like Pac-Man.

❽ Lan Su tranquility

Finish the walk at the **Lan Su Chinese Garden** (p52), located catty-corner at the end of the block on NW Everett St. It's a tranquil place to digest as you admire the traditional Chinese architecture and landscaping – tai chi and kung fu classes are also regularly scheduled.

F1
F

SW Front Ave (Naito Pkwy)

1

2

3
Tom McCall
Waterfront
Park

4
Japanese American ◉ 2
Historical Plaza

Old Town ⊕
Chinatown
E
NW 1st Ave

Lan Su
◉ Chinese Garden

NW 2nd Ave
D
OLD TOWN
CHINATOWN

14 ◉

17 ✪
NW 3rd Ave

1 Shanghai
◉ Tunnels

NW Davis St
C
19 ⊟

18 ⊟
NW Couch St

Chinatown
5 ◉ Gateway

W Burnside St

NW Flanders St

NW Everett St

NW 4th Ave

11 ✕
⊙⊟
13 22

⊟
20

NW Couch
B
NW 5th Ave

21
12 ◉   ◉

NW Davis
A
NW 6th Ave

15 ◉

1

2

3

4

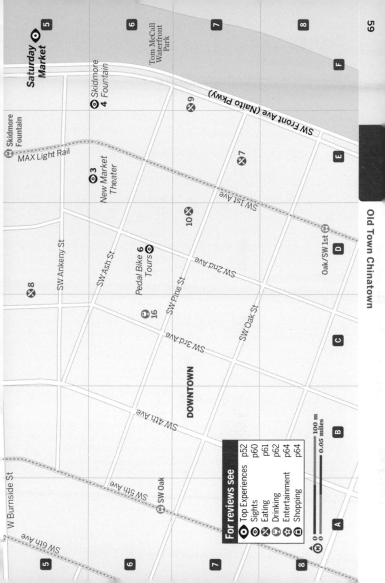

Saturday Market ⦿ 5

⦿ Skidmore
4 Fountain

Tom McCall
Waterfront Park

SW Front Ave (Naito Pkwy)

❌ 9

⦿ Skidmore
Fountain

Ⓜ MAX Light Rail

❌ 7

⦿ 3
New Market
Theater

❌ 10

SW 1st Ave

Ⓜ Oak/SW 1st

SW Ankeny St

SW Ash St

Pedal Bike ⦿
6 Tours

SW 2nd Ave

SW Oak St

❌ 8

⦿ 16

SW Pine St

SW 3rd Ave

SW 4th Ave

DOWNTOWN

W Burnside St

SW 5th Ave

Ⓜ SW Oak

SW 6th Ave

For reviews see	
⦿ Top Experiences	p52
⦿ Sights	p60
❌ Eating	p61
🍷 Drinking	p62
✪ Entertainment	p64
🛍 Shopping	p64

0 ⟶ 100 m
0 ⟶ 0.05 miles

A B C D E F

Sights

Shanghai Tunnels HISTORIC SITE

1 ⊙ MAP P58, C3

Downtown Portland's basements were once connected by tunnels running beneath the streets and down to riverside docks. While they were built for shipping and flood control, rumors persist that they were also used to transport unconscious men to be sold to unscrupulous ship's captains. Most of the tunnels have long been sealed, but remnants can be visited by tour. (☎503-622-4798; 120 NW 3rd Ave; adult/child $13/8; 🚍12, 19, 20, 🚊Blue, Red)

Japanese American Historical Plaza MEMORIAL

2 ⊙ MAP P58, F4

North of the Burnside Bridge, the Japanese American Historical Plaza is a memorial to Japanese Americans who were sent to intern-ment camps by the US govern-ment during WWII. Artwork in the memorial garden depicts the story of the Pacific Northwest's Japanese residents. A bronze and stone sculpture named *Songs of Inno-cence, Songs of Experience* by artist Jim Gion forms the gateway to the plaza. (Tom McCall Waterfront Park)

New Market Theater LANDMARK

3 ⊙ MAP P58, E6

This landmark was built in 1872 and is notable for the cast iron arches facing SW 1st Ave, all that

are left of its northern wing. (50 SW 2nd Ave; 🚊Blue)

Skidmore Fountain FOUNTAIN

4 ⊙ MAP P58, F6

Victorian-era architecture and the attractive Skidmore Fountain give the area beneath the Burnside Bridge some nostalgic flair. Dedi-cated in 1888, the National Historic Landmark site is Portland's oldest piece of public art.

Chinatown Gateway GATE

5 ⊙ MAP P58, B4

Though it was once the second-largest Chinatown in the US, don't expect flashbacks of Shanghai in Portland's Chinese quarter these days – most of its former residents and businesses have moved to outer Southeast neighborhoods. Still, the deceptively impressive pagoda-style Chinatown Gateway remains a beloved local landmark and a symbol of the city's Chinese heritage. (🚍20)

Pedal Bike Tours CYCLING

6 ⊙ MAP P58, D6

Offers all sorts of themes – his-tory, doughnuts, beer – plus day trips to the Columbia Gorge. The three-hour 'bike & boat' pack-age includes a historic bike tour of downtown and a sightsee-ing cruise with Portland Spirit (p42). (☎503-243-2453; www.pedalbiketours.com; 133 SW 2nd Ave; tours from $49; ⊙10am-6pm; 🚍15, 16, 51, 🚊Blue, Red)

Eating

Kalé

JAPANESE CURRY $

7 MAP P58, E7

Kalé does one thing with minimal variation – and does it well. Its homestyle Japanese curry, composed of onions, carrots, garlic, celery and tomatoes, is cooked for two days before finally being served alongside rice and adorned with chicken, beef or veggies. The dining room features bright lights, cheery red accents and a mural of abstract veggies on the wall. (☏503-206-4114; www.kalepdx.com; 50 SW Pine St; curries $9-12; ☉11am-8pm Mon-Thu, to 9pm Fri & Sat)

Voodoo Doughnut

DESSERTS $

8 ✖ MAP P58, D5

There's nothing quite like this standing-room-only hole-in-the-wall (pun intended) spot. It bakes creative, sickly-sweet treats – go for the surprisingly good bacon-maple bar or the 'cock 'n balls' (shaped like a...well, yes). Part of the fun is standing in line with everyone else, and then carrying around that distinctive pink box so people know where you've been. (☏503-241-4704; www.voodoodoughnut.com; 22 SW 3rd Ave; doughnuts from $2; ☉24hr)

Old Town Chinatown Eating

Japanese American Historical Plaza

MOTOKO/SHUTTERSTOCK ©

Weekend Street Party

On weekend nights, several blocks of Old Town Chinatown closes off to vehicular traffic and the area becomes a pedestrians-only zone with the party spilling out into the streets. If you've come to Portland for alcohol-fueled revelry on the dance floor, this is where you'll find it.

LeChon

SOUTH AMERICAN $$

9 🍴 MAP P58, F7

This under-the-radar eatery on the waterfront specializes in South American fare. Dishes from Argentina, Chile, Patagonia and Peru include pork *anticucho* (grilled heart), *lomo saltado* (sirloin strips with rice and fries), empanadas and ceviche. If you're after an extravaganza, try the *asado* (grilled meat) main – flank steak, lamb T-bone, sweetbreads and smoked sausages will stuff you to the gills. (☑503-219-9000; www.lechonpdx.com; 113 SW Naito Pkwy; mains $12-28; ⏱11am-2pm & 4:30-10pm Mon-Thu, to 11pm Fri, 3-11pm Sat, 3-10pm Sun)

Pine Street Market

AMERICAN $$

10 🍴 MAP P58, D7

An indoor food hall in the historic Baggage and Carriage Building downtown, Pine Street Market collects eight buzz-worthy restaurants and cafes around a central dining area, including outlets from the minds behind Salt & Straw (ice cream) and Olympia Provisions (p76). (www.pinestreetpdx.com; 126 SW 2nd Ave; prices vary; ⏱9am-11pm)

Tope

MEXICAN $$

11 🍴 MAP P58, B4

This taqueria and bar on the rooftop of the Hoxton hotel stuns with floor-to-ceiling white tiles, hanging plants, warm wood furnishings and gold accents. Street tacos include *lengua* (tongue), fried rock fish, beef cheek *adobo*, spicy lamb sausage and roasted cauliflower, though the execution of some left us wanting. While you can find better tacos elsewhere, views from here can't be beat. (☑503-770-0500; https://thehoxton.com/portland/tope-restaurant; 15 NW 4th Ave; tacos $5-6, snacks $9-19; ⏱4-10pm Sun & Mon, to 11pm Tue-Thu, to midnight Fri & Sat; ◻20)

Drinking

Ground Kontrol Classic Arcade

BAR

12 MAP P58, A3

Remember Galaga? You can still play it at this awesome video arcade for adults, along with plenty of other vintage arcade games and pinball machines. There's a basic bar food menu as well as beer, wine and cocktails. Check online for 'free play' nights and other events. (📞503-796-9364; www.groundkontrol.com; 115 NW 5th Ave; games 25-50¢; 🕐noon-2:30am; 🚌20, 🚃Green, Orange, Yellow)

Deadstock Coffee   COFFEE

13 🚇 MAP P58, B4

Deadstock's ethos that 'coffee should be dope' comes through in its signature concoctions and blends, such as the LeBronald Palmer (a mix of iced coffee, sweet tea and lemonade) and Fresh Prince (Ethiopian light-roast beans). Owner Ian Williams once worked his way from janitor to shoe designer at Nike HQ, and it's the world's only coffee shop dedicated to sneaker culture. (📞971-220-8727; www.deadstockcoffee.com; 408 NW Couch St; 🕐7:30am-5pm Mon-Fri, 9am-6pm Sat, 10am-4pm Sun)

CC Slaughters   LGBTIQ+

14 🚇 MAP P58, D2

This popular, long-running night-club boasts a big, loud dance floor and good DJs. When you tire of shaking your bootie, head into the relaxed Rainbow Room lounge. There's a Sunday-night drag show and fun themed nights. (📞503-248-9135; www.ccslaughterspdx.com; 219 NW Davis St; 🕐3pm-2:30am)

Silverado   GAY

15 🚇 MAP P58, A4

Expect almost nightly stripper shows at this club catering to men.

It's a mixed crowd with cheap drinks, potential groping and mus-cled dancers – bring plenty of dollar bills and count on a wild time. If you need a breather, there's an outdoor terrace and lounge with a pool table and video poker. (📞503-224-4493; www.silveradopdx.com; 610 NW Couch St; 🕐9pm-2:30am)

Stumptown Coffee Roasters – Downtown   COFFEE

16 🚇 MAP P58, C6

The downtown location of the famous Portland coffee roast-ing empire is the most spacious and has art shows that change monthly. (www.stumptowncoffee.com; 128 SW 3rd Ave; 🕐6am-7pm Mon-Fri, 7am-7pm Sat & Sun; 📶)

Chinatown Gateway (p60)

RITU MANOJ JETHANI/SHUTTERSTOCK ©

Old Town Chinatown Drinking

Sporty Shopping

In the hometown of Nike, you can bet this city is filled with lovers of athletic apparel. Old Town Chinatown is the best place in town to find local retailers who specialize in streetwear, both new and vintage.

Entertainment

Darcelle XV   CABARET

17 ⭐ MAP P58, C2

This is Portland's Vegas-style cabaret show, featuring glitzy drag queens in big wigs, fake jewelry and overstuffed bras. Musical performances are spiced with corny comedy, while hapless audience members are picked out and teased. Male strippers perform at midnight on Friday and Saturday. Reservations aren't required, but recommended for shows Wednesday through Saturday. (☏503-222-5338; www.darcellexv.com; 208 NW 3rd Ave; $20; ☺8pm Wed-Sat, 10:30pm Fri & Sat)

Shopping

Kiriko Made   CLOTHING

18 🅐 MAP P58, C3

For truly one-of-a-kind gifts that also tick the sustainable box, turn to this atelier and boutique that creates clothing, accessories and home goods from vintage Japanese textiles. The owner uses centuries-old traditional dyeing and stitching techniques to reimagine garments like kimonos, dresses, shirts and aprons in a modern aesthetic. (☏503-222-0335; https://kirikomade.com; 325 NW Couch St; ☺10am-6pm Mon-Fri, from noon Sat & Sun)

Laundry   VINTAGE

19 🅐 MAP P58, C3

In a city that's chock-full of great secondhand shopping, Laundry offers something unique, specializing in premium vintage streetwear and sports apparel. You can score old-school Starter jackets, band tees, player jerseys and snap-back caps, plus all the throwback Polo, Tommy Hilfiger and Nautica gear that your '90s self once desired. (www.laundrypdx.com; 140 NW 4th Ave; ☺11am-6pm Mon-Sat, to 5pm Sun)

Orox Leather Goods   FASHION & ACCESSORIES

20 🅐 MAP P58, B4

A love for leather craft spans four generations at family-owned and operated Orox. Their roots are in Oaxaca, but everything is handmade right in the Old Town Chinatown store, which is half showroom and half production workshop. Take in the aroma of raw leather and sewing machine oil as you browse beautiful bags, wallets, shoes, belts and hats. (☏503-954-2593; www.oroxleather.com; 450 NW Couch St; ☺10am-5pm Mon-Sat)

Voodoo Doughnut (p61)

Compound Gallery

CONCEPT STORE

21 MAP P58, A3

Peddling trendy threads, sneakers, backpacks and collectable toys since 2002, this bi-level retailer and gallery is where streetwear hype and Japanese pop-art culture collide. Local and underground designers are showcased alongside big-name brands; it has a boutique Nike account, so you're likely to score coveted, hard-to-find kicks here. Regular community events are hosted in the space. (☎503-796-2733; www.compoundgallery.com; 107 NW 5th & Couch St; ⏰11am-7pm Mon-Thu, to 8pm Sat, noon-6pm Sun)

Floating World Comics

BOOKS

22 MAP P58, B4

An excellent comic bookstore in Old Town, with a vast but well-curated selection ranging from superhero to literary. (☎503-241-0227; www.floatingworldcomics.com; 400 NW Couch St; ⏰11am-7pm)

Explore
Northwest & the Pearl District

Northwest Portland encompasses three distinct neighborhoods all connected by walkable streets. Nob Hill's arts-and-crafts-style storefronts house restaurants and shops amid Victorian homes. Industrial Slabtown is up-and-coming with new high-rise residences, while the once-industrial Pearl District is characterized by its cobblestone streets, old loading docks and boutiques and is now one of the state's chicest neighborhoods.

The Short List

○ **Powell's City of Books (p68)** *Losing yourself to a whole city block of books at the nation's largest independent bookstore.*

○ **Cinema 21 (p71)** *Settling into an independent or foreign flick at Portland's top art-house cinema.*

○ **Barista (p77)** *Stopping for coffee at one of the city's best shops, boasting award-winning baristas.*

○ **Pearl District shopping (p78)** *Browsing blocks of beloved international brands to homegrown hits such as MadeHere PDX, all tax-free.*

○ **Breweries (p77)** *Sipping craft brews at buzzing tap houses like Breakside Brewery.*

Getting There & Around

🚋 All streetcar lines (A Loop, B Loop and NS Line) serve the Pearl District; the NS Line runs from the South Waterfront in the West Hills to NW 23rd St in Nob Hill.

🚌 Route 15 runs from Southeast Portland to Nob Hill, via downtown. Route 20 runs along Burnside St from Southeast Portland to Nob Hill.

Neighborhood Map on p72

Pearl District ARTYOORAN/SHUTTERSTOCK ©

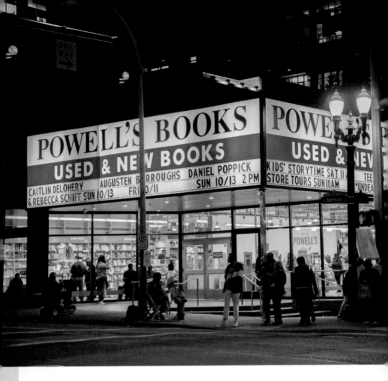

Top Experience 📷
Browse the Stacks at Powell's City of Books

Powell's City of Books is a Portland institution. Occupying five floors and spanning an entire city block, the iconic retailer is the largest independent bookstore in the country. Its nine color-coded rooms house millions of books on every subject imaginable, and with throngs of individuals wandering the stacks each day, it's one of the best places in Portland for people-watching.

◉ MAP P72, G6
📞 800-878-7323
www.powells.com
1005 W Burnside St
🕐 9am-11pm
🚌 20

A Family Affair

Powell's took root in Chicago, where Michael Powell opened his first bookstore in 1970. Michael's father, Walter – a retired painting contractor – spent the summer of 1971 working in the Chicago store. He enjoyed it so much that he opened his own used bookstore upon returning home to Portland.

Walter's operation soon outgrew the original location. Around the time that Michael left Chicago to join Walter in Portland, with his wife and infant daughter, Emily, in tow, the Powells moved things over to the store's current location, a former old car dealership on NW Burnside St.

In 2010 Michael's daughter, Emily, took over operations for Powell's. She saw the store through several initiatives that addressed the changing landscape of book-selling in the digital age. In 2013, Emily stepped away from the family business, but returned as the president and owner in 2019.

Readings & Events

Each month, dozens of authors, artists and thought-leaders visit Powell's for readings, panels and other events in the Pearl Room's Basil Hallward Gallery. The store also hosts children's story hours (some led by drag queens), poetry slams, book clubs, writing workshops and game demonstrations.

Rare Wonders

Powell's **Rare Book Room** (11am to 7pm) is a temple of first-edition collectables and antiquarian treasure. Resembling an old library, the 1000-sq-ft space has antique lamps that cast a warm glow, creating an elegance that's perfect for perusing the 9000-volume collection.

The oldest book is a work by Decimus Magnus Ausonius (310–395 AD) that dates back to 1494. The most expensive is a two-volume set of the first public description of the Lewis and Clark Centennial Exposition, valued at $350,000.

★ Top Tips

○ To wander more strategically, grab a map from the information desk, located in the Green Room.

○ For those who prefer more guidance with their browsing, Powell's offers a staff-led tour of the store at 10am on Sunday. The tour lasts 45 minutes and slots are first-come, first-served.

○ If a tour is too much, there are very helpful staff on each floor who can help you find just about any book you could think of.

✕ Take a Break

Powell's Coffee Room houses a branch of local cafe **World Coffee & Tea** (www.worldcup coffee.com).

There are plenty of eateries within walking distance – **Little Big Burger** (☎503-274-9008; www. littlebigburger.com; 122 NW 10th Ave; burgers $5-6; ☺11am-10pm) for the carnivores, and Prasad (p75) for the herbivores.

Walking Tour 🥾

Nob Hill & Slabtown

In vogue with upper-crust Portlanders since the 1880s, Nob Hill is an upscale residential area filled with stately Victorian homes, trendy restaurants and homegrown boutiques. Slabtown – Portland's most recent up-and-coming district that was once industrial – houses modern high-rise condos and an ever-growing number of restaurants and bars. NW 21st and NW 23rd Aves are the arteries connecting the two districts.

Walk Facts

Start Dragontree Spa
(🚐 15)
End Breakside Brewery
(🚐 15; 🚌 NS)
Length 2 miles; five hours

❶ Spa rejuvenation

Kick things off with an indulgent spa treatment at **Dragontree** (📞503-221-4123; www.thedragontree.com; 2768 NW Thurman St; 1hr massage from $105; 🕙10am-8.15pm Sun-Fri, 9am-9pm Sat) in Slabtown. You'll emerge rejuvenated after a full-body massage – pick from Swedish or deep tissue, with the option of products infused with herbs, essential oils and even CBD; all massages include 30 minutes in the sauna. Body scrubs, facials, Ayurvedic therapies and acupuncture are also available.

❷ Baked treats

Pop into Slabtown's French bakery **St Honoré Boulangerie** (📞503-445-4342; www.sainthonorebakery.com; 2335 NW Thurman St; meals $10-14, pastries $3-6; 🕙7am-8pm) for a post-spa treat. Sample mini marionberry croissants, brioche toast with vanilla and rum custard and fresh apples, and lemon custard tarts with almond cream. Snag a table on the sidewalk and settle into the sweetness.

❸ Elite Ave

Take a stroll down **NW 23rd Ave**, the area's most buzzing street that forms the western border of Nob Hill. It's lined with loads of local businesses housed in arts-and-crafts-style storefronts, where you'll rub shoulders with Portland's elite.

❹ Neighborhood cinema

For a bit of avant-garde entertainment, head to **Cinema 21** (📞503-223-4515; www.cinema21.com; 616 NW 21st Ave) in Nob Hill. It's Portland's top pick for art-house, independent and foreign flicks – all of which you can enjoy with a beer or a glass of wine.

❺ Beer o'clock

Stop by **Breakside Brewery** (p77) in Slabtown for a beer. Renowned for its innovative techniques, many of its brews are laced with exotic fruits and aromatics. The tap house pours craft brews from 16 taps, including its nationally award-winning IPA. The vast space is buzzing with locals, who also enjoy the outdoor patio on a sunny day.

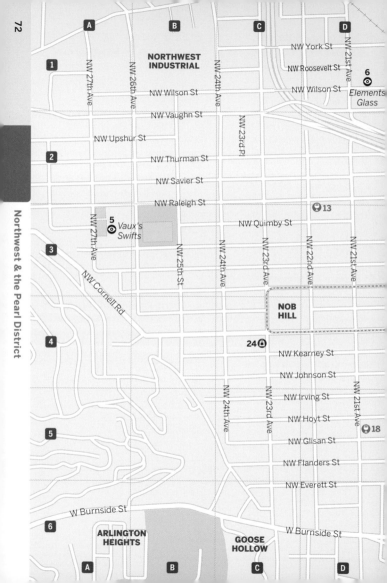

A
B
C
D

1

NW 27th Ave
NW 26th Ave

NORTHWEST INDUSTRIAL

NW 24th Ave

NW York St
NW Roosevelt St

NW 21st Ave

6
Elements Glass

NW Wilson St

NW Wilson St

NW Vaughn St

NW 23rd Pl

2

NW Upshur St

NW Thurman St

NW Savier St

NW Raleigh St

NW Quimby St

13

5 Vaux's Swifts

NW 27th Ave

3

NW Cornell Rd

NW 25th St

NW 24th Ave

NW 23rd Ave

NW 22nd Ave

NW 21st Ave

NOB HILL

4

24

NW Kearney St

NW Johnson St

NW 24th Ave

NW 23rd Ave

NW Irving St

NW 21st Ave

5

NW Hoyt St

18

NW Glisan St

NW Flanders St

NW Everett St

6

W Burnside St

ARLINGTON HEIGHTS

GOOSE HOLLOW

W Burnside St

A
B
C
D

E   F   G   H

NORTHWEST
DISTRICT

For reviews see

◉ Top Experiences   p68
◉ Sights   p74
✗ Eating   p75
🍷 Drinking   p77
★ Entertainment   p78
🔒 Shopping   p78

NW 20th Ave

NW Vaughn St
NW Upshur St

NW 18th Ave

PEARL

⊕N 0 _____ 200 m
    0 _____ 0.1 miles

2

Willamette
River

NW Savier St

✗9

SW Front Ave (Naito Pkwy)

NW 13th Ave

3

PlayDate
PDX
4 ◉

NW Quimby St

3 ◉
Planet
Granite

NW 12th Ave

NW 11th Ave

16
⊕

NW 9th Ave

NW Pettygrove St

NW Overton St

Portland Streetcar
NW Northrup St

NW Marshall St

NW Lovejoy St

Portland Streetcar

NW 15th Ave

NW 14th Ave

✗12

10
⊕

2 Jamison Square
◉ Fountain

4

NW Johnson St

OLD TOWN
CHINATOWN

NW 20th Ave

NW 19th Ave

NW 17th Ave

NW 16th Ave

✗11
NW Irving St

NW Hoyt St

14 ⊕

NW 10th Ave

Center for
Contemporary
Art & Culture

Couch
Park

★19

NW Glisan St

15
⊕

1 ◉

🔒
22

5

NW Flanders St

✗
8

NW Trinity Pl

NW 15th Ave

NW Flanders St

NW Everett St

23
🔒

NW Park Ave

NW 8th Ave

Bolt
Bus

⊕17   ✗7

North Park
Blocks

NW Davis St

20
★

NW Couch St

6

🔒 21

W Burnside St

SW Morrison St

Powell's City
of Books ◉

W Burnside St

SW Oak St

E   F   G   H

Sights

Center for Contemporary Art & Culture
MUSEUM

1 ◉ MAP P72, H5

Home to the 1300-item collection of the former Museum of Contemporary Craft, this exhibition space at PNCA (Pacific Northwest College of Art) focuses on the role of craft and design in modern culture and presents several intriguing exhibitions each year. Check online for events and lectures open to the public. (CCAC; ☎503-226-4391; http://ccac.pnca.edu; 511 NW Broadway; admission free; ⏱11am-6pm Mon-Sat)

Jamison Square Fountain
FOUNTAIN

2 ◉ MAP P72, G4

For simple pleasures, visit the Jamison Square Fountain, a popular Pearl District oasis that attracts splashing kids. (810 NW 11th Ave; 👶; 🚃NS Line, A Loop, B Loop)

Planet Granite
CLIMBING

3 ◉ MAP P72, F3

This enormous indoor rock-climbing gym has something for every level of climber, from total newbie to expert. You'll need a belay partner to climb on the rope routes downstairs, but there's also a huge bouldering area on the 2nd floor, as well as a range of gym equipment. Also runs a full schedule of classes including yoga and Pilates. (☎503-477-5666; www.planetgranite.com; 1405 NW 14th Ave; day pass adult/child $21/15, shoes & harness rental $7; ⏱6am-11pm Mon-Fri, 8am-8pm Sat, to 6pm Sun; 🚃B Loop, NS Line)

PlayDate PDX
PLAYGROUND

4 ◉ MAP P72, F3

A huge indoor playground offering wi-fi and some refreshments. Admission is free after 5pm on Monday. (☎503-227-7529; www.playdatepdx.com; 1434 NW 17th Ave; admission $8-14, half-price under 4yr; ⏱9am-8pm Sun-Thu, to 9pm Fri & Sat; 👶)

Vaux's Swifts
BIRD-WATCHING

5 ◉ MAP P72, A3

Every September, tens of thousands of Vaux's swifts roost for the night in Chapman Elementary School's old brick chimney. Seeing them spiral down in their multitudes, right at sunset, is an unforgettable sight. (www.audubonportland.org/local-birding/swiftwatch; 1445 NW 26th Ave; ⏱dusk)

Elements Glass
ART

6 ◉ MAP P72, D1

Glass-artist wannabes can learn to make their own Christmas ornaments during the holiday season at Portland's largest glassblowing shop, just north of the Pearl District. (☎503-228-0575; www.elementsglass.com; 1979 NW Vaughn St; Christmas ornament class from $40; ⏱10am-5:30pm Mon-Fri)

Eating

Prasad

VEGAN $

7 MAP P72, H6

Prasad's location inside a yoga studio tells you a lot. Healthy, hearty salads, bowls and smoothies come in every shade of green: try the Pride of Portland (brown rice, avocado, scallions, olive oil and sauce, with a green juice) or Endless Summer (zucchini noodles, avocado-pesto cream, tomatoes, spinach, bell pepper and basil). Breakfast options include a tasty maple-chia waffle with vanilla cashew cream. (📞503-224-3993; www.prasadpdx. com; 925 NW Davis St; mains $4-12; ⏰7:30am-8pm Mon-Fri, 9am-8pm Sat & Sun; ✍; 🚌77)

Northwest Art

Northwest Portland is a great place to experience the city's fine art – many top galleries are here, as well as the CCAC. It's also home to Portland's primary theater company, Portland Center Stage (p78), in addition to a couple of great cinemas. Peppered throughout are plenty of green spaces to take respite as you while your way around the super walkable area. The Pearl District hosts the **Art in the Pearl** (www.artinthepearl.com; ⏰Sep) festival each Labor Day weekend.

Jamison Square Fountain

RITU MANOJ JETHANI/SHUTTERSTOCK ©

Pho Van Fresh

VIETNAMESE $

8 MAP P72, G5

This Pearl District outpost of the Pho Van chainlet serves ultra-fresh classic Vietnamese food in a no-nonsense setting. Try one of the many salad roll variations or a big warm bowl of pho. Order at the counter. (📞503-248-2172; www. phovanfresh.com; 1012 NW Glisan St; mains $8-14; ⏱11am-10pm Mon-Sat)

Olympia Provisions

FRENCH $$

9 MAP P72, F2

French-inspired rotisserie bistro serving up charcuterie and cheese boards, gourmet sandwiches, salads and deli items, and main plates such as rotisserie chicken and steamed clams. It also does delicious eggs Benedict for brunch. (📞503-894-8136; www.olympiaprovisions.com; 1632 NW Thurman St; charcuterie $17-34, sandwiches $10-18, mains $17-27; ⏱11am-10pm Mon-Fri, 9am-10pm Sat, 9am-9pm Sun; 🚌16)

Piazza Italia

ITALIAN $$

10 MAP P72, G4

Remember that great *ragù* you last had in Bologna or those memorable *vongole* (clams) you once polished off in Sicily? Well, here they are again at this highly authentic restaurant that succeeds where so many fail: replicating the true essence of Italian food in North America. (📞503-478-0619; www. piazzaportland.com; 1129 NW Johnson St; pasta $12-16; ⏱11:30am-3pm daily, plus 5-9:30pm Sun-Tue, 5-10pm Wed & Thu, 5-11pm Fri & Sat)

Vietnamese chicken and rice noodle bowl

AGAVE PHOTO STUDIO/SHUTTERSTOCK ©

Irving Street Kitchen
MODERN AMERICAN $$$

11 MAP P72, G4

This upscale restaurant serves Pacific Northwest cuisine with a Southern touch, with exceptional dishes like braised beef cheeks with horseradish and parsnip puree. Save room for the butterscotch pudding served in Mason jars. The wine list is also notable. It does brunch too. (☎503-343-9440; www.irvingstreetkitchen.com; 701 NW 13th Ave; mains $21-30; ⏰5:30-10pm Mon-Fri, 10am-2:30pm & 5:30-11pm Sat & Sun)

Café Nell
AMERICAN $$$

12 MAP P72, E4

This little bistro in Nob Hill is both cozy and sophisticated. Large portions of comfort food range from breakfast omelets and oysters on the half shell to wild mushroom risotto and grilled salmon. Happy hour means classic cocktails, frites and tacos. (☎503-295-6487; www.cafenell.com; 1987 NW Kearney; mains $19-26; ⏰11am-10pm Mon-Fri, 9am-10pm Sat, 9am-8pm Sun)

Drinking

Breakside Brewery
BREWERY

13 MAP P72, D3

Breakside is known for experimental brews laced with fruits, vegetables and spices, plus a nationally lauded IPA. Sixteen taps, great grub and two levels of seating (plus a large patio) in a cheery industrial space make it one of Portland's finest brewpubs. (☎503-444-7597; www.breakside.com; 1570 NW 22nd Ave; ⏰11am-10pm Sun-Thu, to 11pm Fri & Sat; 🚌8)

Barista
COFFEE

14 MAP P72, G5

A truly excellent coffee shop, this tiny, stylish shop is owned by award-winning barista Billy Wilson. Beans are sourced from specialty roasters. Three other locations in town. (☎503-274-1211; www.baristapdx.com; 539 NW 13th Ave; ⏰6am-7pm Mon-Fri, from 7am Sat & Sun; 🚌77)

Lowbrow Lounge
BAR

15 MAP P72, G5

A dark, divey oasis holding its ground against the encroaching condo-ization of the neighborhood, the Lowbrow is old-school Portland at its best: weird art, great beer, friendly and unfussy bartenders, better-than-dive-standard food at good prices. If you're meeting someone there, it's fun to arrive first, sit toward the back, and watch your friend stumble in blinded until their eyes adjust to the darkness. (☎503-226-0200; www.lowbrowlounge.com; 1036 NW Hoyt St; ⏰3pm-2:30am Mon-Sat; 🚌77)

Ovation
COFFEE

16 MAP P72, G3

Stop in for a warming Moroccan spice latte at this airy, glassed-in coffee shop, with tempting pastries and friendly staff. Other Moroccan-leaning treats include mint tea and

Easy as A, B, C

Collectively, Nob Hill and Slabtown are referred to as the **Alphabet District**. The street names are in alphabetical order, starting southerly with Burnside St, which spans the entire area, up to northernmost York St in Slabtown. Fans of the *Simpsons* will note some familiar names here (creator Matt Groening is from Portland), such as Flanders, Lovejoy and Quimby Sts.

a pistachio latte. (📞503-719-7716; www.ovationpdx.com; 941 NW Overton St; 🕙6am-6pm Mon-Fri, 7am-5pm Sat & Sun; 🚋NS Loop, B Loop)

Deschutes Brewery   BREWERY

17 🍺 MAP P72, G6

This is a branch of the Bend brewery, but the stuff is brewed here, too – which keeps pints fresh and tasty in all 26 taps. The Mirror Pond Ale and Obsidian Stout have won 'best of show' at the International Brewing Awards, and the Fresh Squeezed IPA is brilliant. (📞503-296-4906; www.deschutesbrewery.com; 210 NW 11th Ave; 🕙11am-10pm, to midnight Fri & Sat)

Sterling Coffee Roasters   COFFEE

18 🍺 MAP P72, D5

Elegant coffee shop roasting complex with flavorful beans. The menu is simple, with great cappuccinos

and espressos by knowledgeable baristas. (📞503-248-2133; www.sterlingcoffeeroasters.com; 518 NW 21st Ave; 🕙6am-5pm Mon-Fri, from 8am Sat & Sun)

Entertainment

Mission Theater   CINEMA

19 ⭐ MAP P72, F5

Come early for a front-row balcony seat at this beautiful McMenamins theater, with mostly second-run movies and lectures. (📞503-223-4527; www.mcmenamins.com; 1624 NW Glisan St)

Portland Center Stage   THEATER

20 ⭐ MAP P72, G6

The city's main theater company performs in the Portland Armory – a renovated Pearl District landmark with state-of-the-art features. (📞503-445-3700; www.pcs.org; 128 NW 11th Ave; tickets from $25; 🚌4, 8, 44, 77)

Shopping

MadeHere PDX   CONCEPT STORE

21 🔒 MAP P72, H6

This expansive shop in the Pearl sources from more than 280 different suppliers, all based in the Pacific Northwest. Everything is made locally, from fancy soaps and luxury chocolates to snowboards, backpacks, leather goods and rugged outdoor clothing. Sales staff know the backstory of each supplier, and there's a definite sense of community. (📞503-224-0122; www.

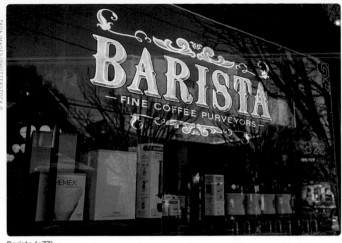

Barista (p77)

madehereonline.com; 40 NW 10th Ave; ⊙11am-6pm Sun-Wed & Fri, to 7pm Thu, 10am-7pm Sat; 🚍20, 🚍B Loop, NS Line)

Thelonius Wines ALCOHOL

22 🔒 MAP P72, H5

A very cute wine shop in the Pearl that doubles as a tasting room, Thelonius was started by an Argentine with a long resume in Pacific Northwest wineries. Like practically everywhere these days, the shop's primary focus is on natural and organic wines. Tastings are scheduled every Friday from 6pm to 8pm and occasionally on Monday and Tuesday. (☎503-444-7747; www.theloniouswines.com; 516 NW 9th Ave; ⊙4-9pm Mon-Fri, noon-9pm Sat, noon-7pm Sun; 🚍77)

Halo Shoes SHOES

23 🔒 MAP P72, H5

Gorgeous, high-end designer shoes for both women and men, with knowledgeable service personnel to go along. You'll need a very fat wallet, but you won't get better-quality shoes. Sells nice handbags, too. (☎503-331-0366; www.haloshoes. com; 938 NW Everett St; ⊙11am-6pm Mon-Sat, noon-5pm Sun)

MudPuddles Toys & Books TOYS

24 🔒 MAP P72, C4

Educational toys and books as well as all the latest for the kids. (☎503-224-5586; www. mudpuddlestoys.com; 2305 NW Kearney St; ⊙10am-6pm Mon-Thu, to 7pm Fri & Sat, 11am-5pm Sun)

Top Experience 📷
Hike Urban Trails at Forest Park

Covering more than 5100 acres on the eastern slope of the Tualatin Mountains is Forest Park, the largest wooded urban park in the US. Flanking Portland's West Hills, its 70-mile network of verdant trails are a great way to witness the grandeur of the Pacific Northwest's forestlands without having to leave the city limits.

📞 503-223-5449

www.forestpark
conservancy.org

🚌 15, 20

Hit the Trails

Connecting top sights like Washington Park, the Audubon Society and Pittock Mansion, Forest Park's Wildwood Trail is an impressive 30-miles long. Rolling through the woods, the trail is intersected by shorter trails, streams, roads and fire lanes.

The Lower MacLeay Trail is good for Forest Park first-timers. Set in a canyon along Balch Creek, it offers an explosion of lush plant life and majestic trees – including the country's tallest fir tree located within an urban area, a 242ft high giant that can be found near the lichen-coated, 1930s Stone House (pictured). The trail is an easy 1.8-mile round trip, and can be accessed via Lower Macleay Park, located at the westernmost end of NW Upshur St in Northwest Portland.

Pittock Mansion

This grand 1914 **mansion** (☏503-823-3623; www.pittockmansion.org; 3229 NW Pittock Dr; adult/child $12/8; ◷10am-4pm late Sep-Dec & Feb-May, 10am-5pm June-late Sep; P) was built by pioneer-entrepreneur Henry Pittock, who revitalized the *Oregonian* newspaper; his wife Georgiana started Portland's annual Rose Festivals. Guided tours are available, but it's also worth visiting the grounds (free) to have a picnic while taking in the spectacular views. The mansion lies along the Wildwood Trail with dozens of miles of connecting trails branching off it.

Wildlife Spotting

Forest Park is a refuge for 62 mammal species, including black-tailed deer, creeping voles, northern flying squirrels, pocket gophers, Roosevelt elk, Pacific jumping mice and more.

More than 112 bird species take refuge in Forest Park's tree canopy, including northern pygmy and great horned owls and hairy woodpeckers.

★ **Top Tips**

o Biking and horseback riding is permitted only on certain trails – check the Forest Park Conservancy (www.forestparkconservancy.org) website.

o The Portland Parks & Recreation (www.portlandoregon.gov/parks) website has a high-resolution trail map available for download.

✕ **Take a Break**

There's nothing in the way of refreshments in the park, but if you find yourself in the vicinity of the **Audubon Society** (☏503-292-6855; www.audubonportland.org; ◷10am-6pm Mon-Sat, to 5pm Sun), the Nature Store sometimes stocks locally made snacks.

★ **Getting There**

Many of the trailheads are only accessible by car. Check the Portland Parks & Recreation website for specific locations.

Explore ◈
Northeast

Northeast Portland is home to some of the city's most vibrant, ethnically diverse communities. A stretch of Alberta St makes up the Alberta Arts District that all host a wealth of restaurants, bars, galleries and boutiques. Neighborhoods like Irvington feature stately historic residences, while north of the city the thoroughfares of Mississippi Ave and N Williams Ave form the Mississippi-Williams District.

The Short List

○ **Alberta Arts District (p84)** *Wandering blocks of galleries and studios alongside creative locals.*

○ **Mississippi-Williams District (p95)** *Checking out up-and-coming bands at places like Mississippi Studios and dining at restaurants in one of Portland's most rapidly developing areas.*

○ **Hollywood Theatre (p95)** *Taking in a film at this art deco movie house, all while eating pizza and sipping a microbrew.*

○ **Coffee shops (p93)** *Cozying up with a strong espresso and a good book at a local java house.*

○ **Breweries (p94)** *Sampling flights of inventive suds at chill neighborhood breweries.*

Getting There & Around

🚆 The MAX light-rail Red, Blue, Green and Yellow lines stop at Rose Quarter Transit Center, located across from the Moda Center. The Red, Blue and Green lines stop at Lloyd Center.

🚌 From the city center, route 8 runs north along NE 15th, with stops at the Lloyd Center and continuing up past Alberta St.

Neighborhood Map on p88

Hollywood Theatre (p95) EQROY/SHUTTERSTOCK ©

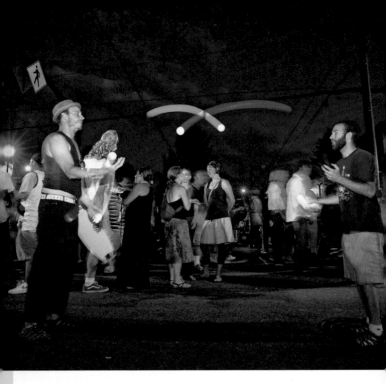

Top Experience 📷
Check Out Local Culture at the Alberta Arts District

👁 MAP P88, D2

In Northeast Portland, the stretch of Alberta St from MLK Jr Blvd to 30th Ave is a corridor of diverse local culture known as the Alberta Arts District. Lined with art galleries, boutiques, restaurants and bars, the main drag is known for its monthly 'Last Thursday' street fair event, but the area is worth exploring any day of the month.

🚌 Route 72 runs along Alberta St from MLK Blvd to NE 30th Ave. From downtown, route 8 travels up 15th Ave and stops at the intersection of Alberta St.

History

Community development task forces were created in 1993 to reinvigorate the Alberta area, which had suffered from disinvestment and segregation for several decades. Focus was placed on providing low-income housing, as well as establishing and empowering neighborhood-oriented and minority-owned small businesses. Artists were drawn to the neighborhood thanks to cheap rents. Residences and studios were set up, and the influx helped spur commercial growth in storefronts that were previously boarded up. By 1997, the neighborhood was home to a thriving creative community.

Last Thursday

Since 1997, the **Last Thursday on Alberta** (pictured; ☎503-823-1052; www.lastthurspdx.org; ⏰6-9pm) art walk has drawn crowds to Alberta St for a dose of creative culture. With buskers, bands, acrobatic troupes and visitors of all stripes, it makes for fantastic people-watching.

Held throughout the year the event ramps up in the summertime. The 15-block stretch of Alberta St (from 15th to 30th Avenues) closes to vehicular traffic from 6pm to 9pm on the last Thursdays of June, July and August. Crowds fill the street as people wander gallery openings and local businesses' art exhibitions. Independent vendors sell their wares along the sidewalks, and there's plenty of food and drink too.

Street Art

Public art adds to the vibrant character of Alberta St, where you'll see bold graffiti, colorful murals, and functional spaces like parking spots reimagined with a creative twist.

The Alberta area was once home to one of the highest populations of African Americans in Portland, who survived a history of segregation and redlining – in addition to today's struggles of gentrification. Much of the public art in this area illustrates realities of this community.

★ Top Tips

○ Alberta St is a prime location for taking in some of Portland's best street art. The Portland Street Art Alliance (www.pdxstreetart. org/finding-street-art) has a free map available for download that features an index of all the street's murals.

✕ Take a Break

Alberta St is peppered with plenty of places to eat. Proud Mary (p93) is a top pick for excellent coffee, fresh juices and smoothies, and Insta-worthy brunch plates.

For great Indian, check out Bollywood Theater (p92). Podnah's Pit (p92), a few blocks away on NE Killingsworth, has some of the best BBQ in the city.

Walking Tour 🚶

Northeast Wellness Walkabout

Northeast Portland is home to locally owned restaurants, shops and galleries, and though it's extremely gentrified, it's also where you'll encounter the most Portlanders from different backgrounds. There are great ethnic eateries along Alberta St, frequented mostly by hip, young creatives, as well as bars with more mellow, hometown vibes.

Walk Facts

Start Green Hop
(🚌 8, 17)

End Beast (🚌 72)

Length 2 miles; six hours

❶ Hip-Hop & weed

Begin this day of wellness at **Green Hop** (☎971-301-5859; www.gogreenhop.com; 5515 NE 16th Ave; ◷8:30am-9:45pm), a dispensary where hip-hop, art and cannabis collide. It's a venture of many firsts: Oregon's first black-owned dispensary, the first co-owned by a black female, and the world's first hip-hop-themed dispensary. Elevate your consciousness with a strain named after a musician, or opt for non-psychoactive CBD gummies to retain a clear head.

❷ Aussie-style avo toast

Make your way to **Proud Mary** (p93), the first US location of the renowned Australian coffee roaster's cafe. For light but filling nosh, order the artfully plated avocado toast. Wash it down with a flat white or other espresso-based drink to get you out the door.

❸ French-pressed fuel

Next, head two blocks east to **Sip**, (☎503-680-5639; www.sipjuicecart.com; 2210 NE Alberta St; drinks $3-8; ◷8am-5pm Mon-Thu, to 6pm Sun), a juice bar housed in a renovated camper van that's permanently parked along Alberta St between 22nd and 23rd Aves. Grab a fresh green or fruit juice to go and down it on your way to the next stop – you'll need to stay plenty hydrated.

❹ Soak & sauna

Spend the next couple of hours at **Common Ground** (☎503-238-1065; www.cgwc.org; 5010 NE 33rd; 1hr soak $17; ◷10am-11pm, last entry 10pm), a co-op with a soaking tub, sauna and a team of wellness providers that specialize in massage, acupuncture, naturopathic medicine and more. All experiences here are clothing-optional, so feel free to let it all hang out if it suits – or bring a suit if it doesn't.

❺ School flicks & chill

Once you're sufficiently relaxed, head to the **Kennedy School Theater** (☎503-249-3983; www.mcmenamins.com; 5736 NE 33rd Ave; adult/child $5/3) for a matinee flick on a comfy sofa. Screening mostly second-run features, this historic theater was once a school auditorium. Unwind even more with a craft beer or a glass of wine. There's pizza and other pub fare if you find yourself peckish, but don't fill up – better eats await.

❻ Save the Beast for last

Finish the day by treating yourself to a six-course feast at **Beast** (p92), featuring a local produce-driven menu that changes every couple of weeks to reflect the Pacific Northwest's best seasonal ingredients.

A B C D

1

N Albina Ave

N Killingsworth St
NE Killingsworth St

17

NE 15th Ave

Alberta Park

10

VERNON

N Alberta St

Everybody's
Bike Rentals
& Tours 2

NE Webster St
NE Alberta St

30

Alberta
Arts
District

14
28

NE Wygant St

King
School
Park

KING

NE Going St

NE Going St

2

NE Prescott St

NE Skidmore St

N Skidmore St

27

SABIN

NE Mason St

NE Mason St

N Mason St

N Shaver St

24
29

31

33

Denorval
Unthank
City Park

BOISE

NE Failing St

NE 13th Ave
NE 15th Ave
NE 17th Ave
NE 19th Ave

3

N Missouri Ave
N Borthwick Ave

16

N Fremont St

9

NE Fremont St

IRVINGTON

N Cook St

Irving
Park

N Mississippi Ave

NE Siskiyou St

N Williams Ave

N Rodney Ave

Matt Dishman
Community
Center & Indoor Pool

NE Knott St

NE 15th Ave
NE 17th Ave
NE 19th Ave

4

N Mississippi Ave

4

Portland's
Culinary
Workshop

NE Knott St 3

NE Russell St

ELIOT

22

Albina/Mississippi

12

NE Thompson St

NE Tillamook St

NE Hancock St

NE Martin Luther King Jr Blvd

5

Willamette
River

Interstate Ave

NE Broadway St

19

NE Hancock St

NE Broadway St

LLOYD

NE Halsey St

32

N Broadway

Rose
Quarter
Transit
Center

23

Holladay
Park

6

Union
Station
(Amtrak)

Interstate
Rose
Quarter

NE 7th

Lloyd Center/
NE 11th

KERNS

NW Hoyt

Greyhound

Oregon
Convention
Center

Convention
Center

1

NE Irving St

A B C D

N

0   500 m
0   0.25 miles

Northeast

E

NE Jarratt St

NE Killingsworth St   ⊗**13**

NE Emerson St

NE Sumner St

⊗**11**

NE Alberta St

⊗**8**

NE Wygant St

NE Going St

NE Prescott St

NE Mason St

NE 30th Ave

ALAMEDA

NE Fremont St

NE Siskiyou St

NE 33rd Ave

NE Knott St

NE Thompson St

NE Hancock St

NE 24th Ave

⊜**18**   NE Schuyler St

**SULLIVAN'S
GULCH**

F

26
🔒

NE Killingsworth St

NE Emerson St

NE Alberta Ct

NE Going St

NE 33rd Ave

Wilshire
Park

NE Shaver St

**BEAUMONT-
WILSHIRE**

NE 33rd Ave

NE Stanton St

US
Grant **5** *Grant*
Park ◉ *Outdoor Pool*
NE Thompson St

**GRANT
PARK**

NE US Grant Pl

25
🔒

NE Broadway St

LAURELHURST

NE 33rd Ave

Banfield Expy

NE Sandy Blvd

Oregon
Park

G

For reviews see

◉	Top Experiences	p84
◉	Sights	p90
⊗	Eating	p90
⊜	Drinking	p93
★	Entertainment	p95
🔒	Shopping	p96

⊗**6**   **CULLY**

NE 42nd Ave

NE Prescott St

NE 42nd Ave

NE Fremont St

NE 41st Ave

NE Klickitat St

NE Siskiyou St

NE Stanton St

NE 42nd Ave

NE Brazee St **20**
⊜

**ROSE
CITY
PARK**

15 ⊜

NE Sandy Blvd

★**21**
7⊗   NE Broadway St
HOLLYWOOD
NE Halsey St

Hollywood
Transit
Center

NE César E Chávez Blvd

H

1

2

Rose City
Cemetery

3

4

5

NE 47th Ave

Frazer
Park

6

E   **F**   **G**   **H**

Sights

Oregon Convention Center
NOTABLE BUILDING

1 ⊙ MAP P88, B6

Those two glass spires you can see from downtown identify this huge multipurpose building where some of Portland's largest events are held. Check the website for a calendar. (www.oregoncc.org; 777 NE Martin Luther King Jr Blvd; ☒Red, Blue, Green, Yellow)

Everybody's Bike Rentals & Tours
CYCLING

2 ⊙ MAP P88, B2

It's true that Portland is best seen by bicycle, and this company offers low-key, fun tours of the city and its surroundings – whether you're into food and farms or beer and parks. Try the 'Beyond Portlandia' tour for an off-the-beaten-path glimpse of the city. Bicycle rentals, from commuters to mountain bikes, are also available. (☎503-358-0152; www.pdxbikerentals.com; 305 NE Wygant St; rentals per hour $8-25, tours per person from $39; ⊙10am-5pm; ☒6)

Matt Dishman Community Center & Indoor Pool
SWIMMING

3 ⊙ MAP P88, B4

Swimmers should grab their suits and make a beeline to the indoor pool here; it's just north of the Lloyd District. Check hours beforehand. (☎503-823-3673; www.portland oregon.gov/parks/60933; 77 NE Knott St; drop-in visit adult/child $6/4)

Portland's Culinary Workshop
COOKING

4 ⊙ MAP P88, A4

From beginner to professional cooking courses, including seafood, barbecuing, Mexican, Thai, gluten-free, pastries and cakes. (☎503-512-0447; www.portlandsculinary workshop.com; 807 N Russell St; per person from $65)

Grant Outdoor Pool
SWIMMING

5 ⊙ MAP P88, F4

There's an outdoor swimming pool at US Grant Park. The pool is only open in summer; check online for exact dates. (☎503-823-3674; www.portlandoregon.gov/parks/61021; 2300 NE 33rd Ave; adult/child $4.75/3.75; ⊙Jun-Sep; ☒70)

Eating

Yonder
SOUTHERN US $

6 ⊗ MAP P88, G2

Yonder's excellent fried chicken is available 'dusted' (adorned with dry spice), 'dipped' (tossed in a zesty sauce) or 'hot' (just spicy enough to be memorable, without injury), served with cornbread or a biscuit with sweet sorghum butter. Add a side of pimento mac and cheese or bacon braised collard greens, then wash it down with a craft cocktail. Down-home good! (☎503-444-7947; www.yonderpdx.com; 4636 NE

42nd Ave; mains $8-17; ⊘11am-9pm Wed-Sun)

Chin's Kitchen

CHINESE $

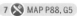 7 ✖ MAP P88, G5

Not so long ago, Chin's was known mostly for its iconic neon sign. But under new owners – two sisters from the city of Harbin in northern China – the humble restaurant has been churning out dumplings to die for. There are also hand-pulled noodles, stews and other well-executed regional dishes making local critics swoon. (☎503-281-1203; www.portlandchinskitchen.com; 4132 NE Broadway; mains $10-16; ⊘11:30am-2:30pm & 5-9pm; 🚊Red, Blue)

Pine State Biscuits

SOUTHERN US $

 8 ✖ MAP P88, E2

Immensely popular for its hangover-sopping fried chicken, bacon and cheese biscuit sandwiches, with egg and gravy additions for the strong of heart. Plenty of sides, with interesting drinks like local apple cider or gourmet chocolate milk. (☎503-477-6605; www.pinestatebiscuits.com; 2204 NE Alberta St; biscuit sandwiches $6-11; ⊘7am-3pm)

Akadi PDX

AFRICAN $$

9 ✖ MAP P88, B3

Akadi chef-owner Fatou Ouattara brings the flavors of her native Ivory Coast and other West African

Oregon Convention Center

Diverse Eats

As the city's most culturally diverse area, Northeast Portland features some of the best ethnic food in town. From food carts to atmospheric neighborhood eateries, you'll find everything from hand-pulled Chinese noodles to West African staples like jolof rice. Many top-rated fine-dining establishments are also located here, offering world-class culinary experiences with a side of hometown charm.

countries to Portland, where you'll find devoted locals enjoying authentic dishes at kente-cloth-covered tables in the low-key dining room. Samusas, cassava sticks, and jolof rice plates are crowd-pleasing entry points, but the flavor-rich traditional stews (eaten with fufu) are truly where it's at. (📞503-477-7138; www.akadipdx.com; 3601 NE Martin Luther King Jr Blvd; mains $13-19; ⏰noon-10pm Tue-Sun)

Podnah's Pit

BARBECUE $$

10 ❌ MAP P88, D1

Possibly Portland's best barbecue joint, serving amazingly tender and tasty pork ribs that have been smoked for four hours. There's also brisket, chicken and pulled-pork sandwiches, along with typical sides such as coleslaw, potato salad and collard greens. (📞503-281-3700; www.podnahspit.com; 1625 NE Killingsworth St; mains $14-32; ⏰11am-9pm Mon-Thu, to 10pm Fri, 9am-10pm Sat, 9am-9pm Sun; 🚌8)

Bollywood Theater

INDIAN $$

11 ❌ MAP P88, E1

This popular Indian restaurant serves up 'street food' such as lamb samosas and *kati* rolls (meat and chutney rolled up in flatbread), along with small plates (chicken curry, pork vindaloo) and *thalis* (traditional set meals of various dishes). Plenty of vegetable and side dishes as well; wash it all down with a chai, a yogurt *lassi* or an Indian cocktail. (📞971-200-4711; www.bollywoodtheaterpdx.com; 2039 NE Alberta St; small plates $11-15, thalis $17-20; ⏰11am-10pm; 🔧; 🚌72)

Ox

STEAK $$$

12 ❌ MAP P88, B5

One of Portland's most popular restaurants is this upscale, Argentine-inspired steakhouse. Start with the smoked bone-marrow clam chowder, then go for the gusto: the grass-fed beef rib eye. If there's two of you, the *asado* (barbecue grill; $94) is a good choice, allowing you to try several different cuts. Reserve ahead. (📞503-284-3366; www.oxpdx.com; 2225 NE Martin Luther King Jr Blvd; mains $14-56; ⏰5-10pm Sun-Thu, to 11pm Fri & Sat; 🚌6)

Beast

AMERICAN $$$

13 MAP P88, F1

At Beast, celebrated local chef Naomi Pomeroy – who went from staging underground supper-club dinners to appearing on *Top Chef* and winning a James Beard Award – offers a set fixed-price menu of six courses, wine pairings optional. Dining here is an event. Expect wildly creative use of carefully sourced ingredients, and a lot of meat. Reserve ahead. (☎503-841-6968; www.beastpdx.com; 5425 NE 30th Ave; dinner without/with wine $118/168, brunch $40/60; �YDinner 6pm & 7:30pm Wed & Thu, 6pm & 8:45pm Fri & Sat, 7pm Sun, brunch 10am, 11:30am & 1pm Sun; 📵72)

Drinking

Proud Mary

CAFE

14 🍷 MAP P88, D2

From the land of flat whites and avocado toast comes Proud Mary, the notable Melbourne-based coffee roaster that aptly chose Portland for its first US outpost. In addition to superb coffee, it slings delicious breakfast, brunch and lunch plates like vanilla and ricotta hotcakes, a smoked pork-belly satay sandwich and Aussie meat pies. Smoothies and fresh juices, too. (☎503-208-3475; www.proudmarycoffee.com; 2012 NE Alberta St; �8am-4pm Mon-Fri, from 8am Sat & Sun)

Breakfast bowl

Moon & Sixpence   PUB

15 🚉 MAP P88, G5

Topping the short list of places in Portland where you can get a proper pint of Guinness is this lovely old-fashioned pub, with good fish-and-chips, friendly but not overly attentive service, darts in the back, old books to borrow, and a huge patio outside for when the rain lets up. On a gray Portland day it's hard to do better. (2014 NE 42nd Ave; ⏱3pm-2:30am)

Ecliptic Brewing   BREWERY

16 🚉 MAP P88, A3

It's in kind of a chilly industrial space, but the beer speaks for itself – Ecliptic was founded by John Harris, who previously brewed for McMenamins, Deschutes and Full Sail. The brewery's astronomically named creations (such as the Craft Beer medal-winning Spica Pilsner) are ambitious and wildly successful. Food includes lamb picatta, tempura asparagus and a goat's cheese and beet melt sandwich. (📞503-265-8002; www.eclipticbrewing.com; 825 N Cook St; ⏱11am-10pm Sun-Thu, to 11pm Fri & Sat; 🚌4)

Saraveza   BREWERY

17 🚉 MAP P88, A1

Saraveza is a bottle shop and pub best known for its American craft beer, served by award-winning 'beertenders.' Choose from over 250 bottles of the stuff, including nine on draft. Also good for its savory and sweet pasties (hand pies). (📞503-206-4252; www.saraveza.com; 1004 N Killingsworth St; ⏱11am-midnight)

Hale Pele   BAR

18 🚉 MAP P88, E5

The kitschy tiki bar (aren't they all?) to come to for 'historical' tropical cocktails, all made from fresh juices, handcrafted syrups and premium spirits. Try the popular Suffering Bastard, made with ginger beer, bourbon, gin and lime. (📞503-662-8454; www.halepele.com; 2733 NE Broadway; ⏱4pm-close)

Upright Brewing   BREWERY

19 🚉 MAP P88, B5

This basement brewery has an intimate tasting room for sampling French and Belgian farmhouse-inspired ales. (www.uprightbrewing.com; 240 N Broadway, Suite 2; ⏱4:30-9pm Thu & Fri, 1-8pm Sat & Sun)

Laurelwood Brewing Co   BREWERY

20 🚉 MAP P88, H4

The rare brewpub that's actively kid-friendly, Laurelwood makes an excellent line of beers, especially the Free Range Red and the IRA. There's a small deck upstairs in good weather, and decent pub grub. Also at 6716 SE Milwaukie Ave and inside Portland airport. (📞503-282-0622; www.laurelwoodbrewpub.com; 5115 NE Sandy Blvd; ⏱11am-10pm; 👶; 🚌12)

Entertainment

Hollywood Theatre
CINEMA

21 MAP P88, G5

This historic art deco cinema has excellent programming, with classic, foreign and quirky independent movies and a reverence for film over digital – it's the only place in town capable of showing movies in 70mm. Several great monthly series, including Queer Horror, B-Movie Bingo and the awesome Kung Fu Cinema, screen rare 35mm classics. There's also pizza and other grub available, plus craft beer on tap to wash it all down. (503-493-1128; www.hollywoodtheatre.org; 4122 NE Sandy Blvd)

Wonder Ballroom
LIVE MUSIC

22 MAP P88, B4

Great live-music venue with good sound quality, excellent lineup of bands and a tiny cafe downstairs. (www.wonderballroom.com; 128 NE Russell St)

Moda Center
STADIUM

23 MAP P88, B6

Formerly named the Rose Garden, this large arena is home to Portland's professional basketball team, the Trail Blazers. (503-235-8771; www.rosequarter.com/venue/moda-center; 1 N Center Court St; Yellow)

Portland Winterhawks
SPECTATOR SPORT

Beervana's major-junior hockey team usually plays at the Moda

Portland Winterhawks

Center. (503-238-6366; www.winterhawks.com; from $35)

Trail Blazers
SPECTATOR SPORT

Rip City's major league basketball team plays at the Moda Center. (www.nba.com/blazers; from $38)

Mississippi Studios
LIVE MUSIC

24 MAP P88, A3

This intimate bar is good for checking out budding acoustic talent along with more established musical acts. Excellent sound system. Located right on busy N Mississippi Ave.

The venue's adjacent Bar Bar pours drinks and serves awesome burgers from 11am to 2am, seven days a week. (503-288-3895; www.mississippistudios.com; 3939 N Mississippi Ave; 4)

Shopping

Ray's Ragtime   VINTAGE

25 🔒 MAP P88, G5

After 30 years in its downtown location this beloved vintage clothing store was on the brink of closing due to rent increases – but it relocated instead. Its inventory is heavy on the '40s through '70s, and the owner has a background in theater – many of his customers are film and TV stylists – so you know the quality is tops. (☏503-226-2616; www.raysragtimehollywood.com; 4059 NE Sandy Blvd; ⏰noon-8pm Mon-Sat, 1-6pm Sun; 🚌12)

Uplift Botanicals   DISPENSARY

26 🔒 MAP P88, F1

You can buy edibles, tinctures and pre-rolled marijuana cigarettes, plus the 'tools of the trade,' at this friendly and unintimidating shop just off Killingsworth. (☏971-319-6118; www.upliftbotanicals.com; 5421 NE 33rd Ave; ⏰9am-10pm)

Paxton Gate   ARTS & CRAFTS

27 🔒 MAP P88, A2

A warning to the squeamish: a snarling fox, a smiling warthog and a gape-mouthed hippo are just a few of the stuffed animals lining the walls here, but this curio shop is not to be missed. Celebrating a fascination with the natural world rather than the desire to capture it, this shop has everything from fossilized mollusks to vintage boiling flasks.

Taxidermy specimens are also for sale, but the shop assures its customers that these items have sourced from animals that have died from natural causes or were humanely euthanized to manage wild populations. (☏503-719-4508; www.paxtongate.com; 4204 N Mississippi Ave; ⏰11am-7pm; 🚌4)

Community Cycling Center   SPORTS & OUTDOORS

28 🔒 MAP P88, D2

You can feel good about shopping at this community bicycle shop, which has a series of programs and classes to help cyclists – especially kids – become competent riders and mechanics. Used bikes, parts and accessories are for sale, and there's a repair shop. (☏503-287-8786; www.communitycyclingcenter.org; 1700 NE Alberta St; ⏰10am-7pm)

Land   GIFTS & SOUVENIRS

29 🔒 MAP P88, A3

Land sells unique, fun and crafty gifts like tote bags, coffee mugs, greeting cards and prints, plus there's an art gallery upstairs. Famous as the setting for the *Portlandia* 'Put a Bird on It' skit. (☎503-451-0689; www.landpdx.com; 3925 N Mississippi Ave; ☉10am-6pm)

Frock Boutique   CLOTHING

30 🏠 MAP P88, D1

One of Alberta St's most whimsical and eclectic clothing stores, Frock Boutique stocks screen-printed T-shirts, sundresses, woolen hats, patterned socks, jewelry, onesies for babies and more (even for the guys). (☎503-595-0379; www.frockboutique. com; 1439 NE Alberta St; ☉10am-6pm Tue-Sat, to 5pm Sun & Mon)

Flutter   GIFTS & SOUVENIRS

31 🏠 MAP P88, A3

This cool N Mississippi Ave shop sells reclaimed and refurbished items for the home, vintage jewelry, birdcages, gothic wedding gowns, ornate pillows and feathery hats. (☎503-288-1649; www.flutter clutter.com; 3948 N Mississippi Ave; ☉11am-7pm Mon-Wed, to 8pm Thu & Fri, 10am-8pm Sat, 10am-7pm Sun)

Broadway Books   BOOKS

32 🏠 MAP P88, D5

A good general, independent bookstore with especially strong literary fiction, biography and nonfiction sections. Holds frequent author readings. (☎503-284-1726; www. broadwaybooks.net; 1714 NE Broadway; ☉10am-7pm Mon-Sat, to 5pm Sun)

Pistils Nursery   ARTS & CRAFTS

33 🏠 MAP P88, A3

Looking for your next terrarium? Something to spruce up your rooftop beehive? This N Mississippi Ave shop has everything for the urban homesteader. Peruse what's needed to create your own farm oasis, including exotic plants, terrariums and accessories. If all the flora sparks ambitions for exercising your green thumb, ask about workshops and in-store events. (☎503-288-4889; http:// pistilsnursery.com; 3811 N Mississippi Ave; ☉10am-7pm)

Walking Tour 🚶

Kerns: The In-Between Zone

Nestled between the city's Northeast and Southeast quadrants, this in-between district blends industrial grit with quaint, hyperlocal charm. New apartment builds, arts-and-crafts multiplexes and single-family bungalows house a mix of residents, and shops and restaurants dot the main drags, from the northern side of E Burnside St up to NE Glisan St and Sandy Blvd, all connected by bustling NE 28th.

Walk Facts

Start Screen Door (🚌 20)

End LaurelThirst Public House (🚌 19)

Length 1.2 miles; seven hours

❶ Brave the brunch line

If you can actually get through the door at **Screen Door** (📞503-542-0880; www.screendoorrestaurant.com; 2337 E Burnside St; mains $9-15; ⏰8am-2pm & 5:30-10pm Mon-Fri, 9am-2:30pm & 5:30-10pm Sat, to 9pm Sun), you ought to feel accomplished. One of Portland's longest brunch lines is worth enduring for excellent plates of Southern-fried decadence. Fried chicken and waffles, biscuits and gravy, shrimp and grits, praline bacon waffles and more will stick to your ribs all day.

❷ Quirky gifts

Burn off brunch with a walk up NE 28th Ave to **ZimZim** (p115), a gift shop that sells items by independent makers. Peddling quirky apparel, hilarious tchotchkes and pop-culture novelties, it's a great place for souvenirs with local character, like a 'Straight Outta Portland' tee or a book on the city's best places to pee.

❸ Beer tasting

Continue up NE 28th Ave to NE Glisan St and take a right to **Migration Brewing** (p112). With reclaimed wood and galvanized steel fixtures, the casual-industrial atmosphere is an inviting space for a round of craft brews. Enjoy sports on the screens inside, or take a seat at one of the many outdoor tables if the weather permits.

❹ Wine time

From the brewery, take a left and continue down Glisan to **Pairings** (p115). Touting itself as a 'wine-geek-speak-free zone,' it takes pride in its designation as Portland's weirdest wine shop. It specializes in pairing wine with foods – but also with dog breeds, astrological signs and songs. Many of its bottles are organic, and it hosts events and classes.

❺ Munchies & mani-pedis

Situated along busy Sandy Blvd,the **Zipper** (www.facebook.com/thezipperpdx; 2705 NE Sandy Blvd; most dishes $6-12; ⏰11am-late; 🚌12) is a modern food court in an architecturally intriguing space with plenty of outdoor seating. Look out for Basilisk, serving up one of Portland's best fried-chicken sandwiches. There's also a great nail salon called Finger Bang, open for late-night mani-pedis.

❻ Live tunes

Close out the evening with live music at the bustling **LaurelThirst Public House** (📞503-232-1504; www.laurelthirst.com; 2958 NE Glisan St; ⏰4pm-midnight Mon & Tue, to 1am Wed & Thu, to 2am Fri, 11am-2am Sat, 11am-midnight Sun). It's one of Portland's oldest independent live-music venues, hosting local acoustic acts mostly in the realm of bluegrass, folk and Americana. Most music is free nightly between 6pm and 8pm; later evening shows may have a small cover.

Explore
Southeast

Southeast Portland ranges from ultra-hip areas like Hawthorne to the up-and-coming like Foster-Powell. It swarms with busy street life and is replete with indie shops, acclaimed restaurants and fun bars. If that's not your scene, there are also some of the loveliest and most peaceful parks in the city.

The Short List

○ **Breweries (p112)** *Sampling craft suds at a range of tap houses like Hopworks Urban Brewery.*

○ **Top chef eats (p108)** *Making the rounds at numerous eateries helmed by Portland's culinary darlings, including Gabriel Rucker's Canard.*

○ **Doug Fir Lounge (p114)** *Catching touring and local indie bands in a subterranean venue with futuristic log-cabin decor.*

○ **Oregon Museum of Science & Industry (p108)** *Seeing science spring to life through interactive exhibits, lab demonstrations and a world-class planetarium.*

○ **Crystal Springs Rhododendron Garden (p108)** *Admiring a symphonic display of 2000 rhododendrons and azaleas at peak bloom.*

Getting There & Around

🚌 Routes 2, 12, 14, 15, 19 and 20 connect the city center with Southeast via its major thoroughfares.

🚃 The A Loop and B Loop streetcar lines connect with downtown via OMSI and Northeast via the convention center.

Neighborhood Map on p106

Crystal Springs Rhododendron Garden (p108)
TOMAS NEVESELY/SHUTTERSTOCK ©

Top Experience 📷
Sample Craft Beer in Beervana

Portland's 'Beervana' nickname is well earned, thanks to some 80 craft breweries in the city limits – more than anywhere in the world. The scene has been going strong since the 1980s, leaving beer lovers spoiled for choice. You can experience the best of Beervana in the Southeast quadrant's walkable neighborhoods, where great tasting rooms, brewpubs and bottle shops abound.

🚊 Southeast Portland is served by a number of routes; key ones include 2, 12, 14, 15, 19 and 20.

Blame it on the Water

Portland's fantastic craft beer begins with Oregon's delicious water, which is supplied by the Bull Run watershed in Mt Hood National Forest with rainfall, fog drip and snowmelt. Unspoiled forestland serves as a natural reservoir that absorbs, stores, filters and eventually releases water into pure streams. Unfiltered and unfluoridated, the water supply is minimally treated before it flows from city taps.

Styles to Sample

In a beer landscape as saturated as Portland's, breweries must hustle to concoct brews that stand out. Expect to try anything from aggressive IPAs to ages-old European-style ales, and everything in between.

The city's most authentic English pub, Horse Brass (pictured left; p113) pours from rare kegs and is the place for hand-pumped, cask-conditioned ales.

Cascade Brewing Barrel House (p112) is the city's prime pick for sour beers – you're guaranteed to pucker up with any pour from its 28 taps.

Crafting especially unusual brews, Hair of the Dog Brewing (p112) uses a technique called 'bottle conditioning,' where several of its beers are re-fermented in the bottle. The result is a boost in alcohol content and complex flavor, as the beer continues to age like fine wine.

Brew-&-View Theaters

If you're torn between catching a movie or sampling microbrews, you can do both simultaneously at Portland's 'brew-and-view' theaters. Southeast is home to some of the city's best, including the Hawthorne Theatre (p115), the Laurelhurst Theater (p114) and the Bagdad Theater (p114) – all wonderful, historic venues that screen a range of flicks to watch while you sip craft suds.

★ Top Tips

o Tasting rooms are a great way to sample several brews at once – but they're typically only open during the day and don't serve food, so plan accordingly.

o Though its neighborhoods are extremely walkable, Southeast is still an expansive area. Biking with a buzz isn't wise, so use the bus or a rideshare to get from district to district.

✕ Take a Break

With Southeast's many brewpubs, you can line your stomach and give your liver a break without having to change venues. Hopworks Urban Brewery (p112) has a vast selection of beer styles on tap to pair with its excellent food menu.

Walking Tour 🥾

The Best of Division-Clinton

Once a sleepy thoroughfare through a residential area, Division St has evolved into one of Portland's hippest drags over the last decade and is still rapidly developing. Several of the city's nationally acclaimed eateries and drinking establishments stretch along the main artery. Parallel and two blocks south, Clinton St features ultra-local hangouts nestled alongside beautiful modern and period homes.

Walk Facts

Start Broder (🚊2, 4)
End Ava Gene's (🚊2, 4)
Length 2 miles; six hours

❶ Scandi brunch

Begin the day at **Broder** (☎503-736-3333; www.broderpdx.com; 2508 SE Clinton St; mains $7-15; ☺8am-3pm), a cozy neighborhood cafe on Clinton St with Scandinavian breakfast fare like fluffy egg scrambles. Breakfast boards feature house-cured gravlax, rye bread, cheese, beet-pickled hard-boiled eggs and granola parfaits. Finish with *æbleskiver* (crispy Danish pancake balls served with tart lemon curd and lingonberry jam).

❷ Spa indulgence

Let the Scandinavian theme continue with a trip to **Loyly** (☎503-236-6850; www.loyly.net; 2713 SE 21st Ave; 2hr sauna visit from $26; ☺10am-9pm), a chic spa facility just off Clinton St with a cedar sauna and steam room. It offers spa and bodywork treatments such as Swedish massages and holistic facials, which you can bundle with sessions in the sauna.

❸ Daily bread

Make your way to **Little T American Baker** (☎503-238-3458; www.littletbaker.com; 2600 SE Division St; mains $6-9; ☺7am-5pm Mon-Sat, 8am-2pm Sun) on Division St for a tea or java-based pick-me-up to prod you back into reality. Nosh on the best baguette in town, or grab a baked goodie like a pear Danish or chocolate-praline croissant to take and enjoy.

❹ Urban brews

Wander through the neighborhood to **Hopworks Urban Brewery** (p112) on Powell St. Admire the lovely arts-and-crafts homes as you walk south down SE 31st Ave, then cross over Powell St and take a right – the brewery will be on the left side. HUB specializes in all-organic beers; try the hazy or citrus IPAs.

❺ Save space for Italian

Award-winning trattoria **Ava Gene's** (☎971-229-0571; www.avagenes.com; 3377 SE Division St; mains $25-35; ☺5-10pm Mon-Thu, to 11pm Fri, 4:30-11pm Sat, 4:30-10pm Sun) features a Roman-inspired menu that utilizes local, seasonal produce and Pacific Northwest–raised meats. Simple yet exceptional dishes include rustic vegetable plates with aromatic finishings and house-made pastas, which can also be served family-style. A creative cocktail menu and an extensive selection of Italian spirits round out an authentic experience. Reserve in advance!

Southeast

A **B** **C** **D**

LLOYD

1

NE Lloyd Blvd
Banfield Expy

NE Oregon St **14**
NE Irving St

NE Glisan St

NE Sandy Blvd

34

Buckman
Field

BUCKMAN

Burnside
Bridge

E Burnside St

16
NE Couch St

SE Ankeny St

2

Eastbank
Esplanade

7 **23**
8 **26**

15
SE Pine St

4
FH Steinbart Co

SE Grand Ave

NE Grand Ave

SE Martin Luther King Jr Blvd

Morrison
Bridge

32

13
SE Stark St

SE Stark St

28

Lone Fir
Cemetery

SE Alder St

SE Morrison St

3

19
SE Yamhill St

18
SE Belmont St

SE Morrison St

22

Hawthorne
Bridge

11

Colonel
Summers
Park

SE Water Ave

SE Grand Ave

SE Hawthorne Blvd

6

4 Oregon Museum
of Science & Industry

SE Market St

3

Marquam
Bridge

OMSI SE Water

HOSFORD-
ABERNETHY

LADD'S
ADDITION

5

Willamette
River

SE Division St

Clinton/SE
12th

SE Clinton St

6

SE Powell Blvd

SE Pershing St

Ross
Island

Oaks Bottom
Wildlife Refuge

2
29

BROOKLYN

SE 17th
& Rhine

Banfield Expy

E
Oregon Park
NE 31st Ave
F
NE 32nd Ave
NE Glisan St
G
NORTH TABOR
NE Glisan St
NE 47th Ave
H

1

NE 28th Ave
9 ⊗ 17
NE Flanders St
NE Everett St
NE Flanders St
NE Couch St

🔒 31
NE Couch St
24 ✲
⊗ 12
E Burnside St
NE 39th Ave
E Burnside St
🔒 33

SE 28th Ave
SE 30th Ave
⊗ 10
SE Pine St
Laurelhurst Park

2

SE 47th Ave

27
SE Stark St
Mazamas
5 ◉
SE 43rd Ave
MT TABOR

SE Belmont St
SE 32nd Ave
SE 33rd Ave
SE 34th Ave
SE Belmont St
21
SE Yamhill St

3

SE Taylor St
SUNNYSIDE
SE Salmon St

SE Main St
SE César E Chávez Blvd

SE Hawthorne Blvd
25 ✲
⊗ 30
SE Hawthorne Blvd
SE Clay St

SE 38th Ave

4

Seawallcrest Park
SE 50th Ave
SE Harrison St
SE Lincoln St

SE 20th Ave
SE 30th Ave
SE 32nd Pl
SE 34th Ave
SE 37th Ave
SE Sherman St

SE Division St
RICHMOND
SE Division St

5

SE Clinton St
SE 31st Ave

SE Woodward St

SE 36th Ave
SE César E Chávez Blvd

Ⓝ
0 ───── 500 m
0 ───── 0.25 miles

SE Franklin St

Crystal Springs Rhododendron Garden
1 ◉

20

SE Powell Blvd
Creston Park

E
F
G
H

For reviews see
◉	Sights	p108
⊗	Eating	p108
⊖	Drinking	p111
✲	Entertainment	p114
🔒	Shopping	p115

Southeast

Sights

Crystal Springs Rhododendron Garden
GARDENS

1 ⊙ MAP P106, E6

The large, beautiful grounds at this 5-acre garden near Reed College are covered with more than 2000 full-grown rhododendrons, azaleas and other plants, and there's a lagoon that's dotted with baby ducks in spring. Most of the garden is in bloom from late March or early April, peaking in May and continuing all summer. (☎503-771-8386; 5801 SE 28th Ave; Oct-Feb free, Mon free, Tue-Sun Mar-Sep $5; ☉dawn-dusk; ⚑; ☐19)

Oaks Bottom Wildlife Refuge
WILDLIFE RESERVE

2 ⊙ MAP P106, B6

Located in Sellwood, this large wetland of around 140 acres has a hiking trail through it, which connects with the nearby Springwater Corridor paved bike path. There's also good bird-watching – you can spot herons, egrets, hawks, osprey, hummingbirds, woodpeckers, falcons, vultures and more. (SE Sellwood Blvd & SE 7th Avenue)

Oregon Museum of Science & Industry
MUSEUM

3 ⊙ MAP P106, A4

This excellent museum offers hands-on science exhibits for kids, along with other temporary exhibits like 'The Science Behind Pixar.' There's also a movie theater, planetarium shows and a submarine tour (all carry a separate charge). Parking costs $5. (OMSI; ☎503-797-4000; www.omsi.edu; 1945 SE Water Ave; adult/child $14.50/10; ☉9:30am-7pm Jun-Aug, to 5:30pm Tue-Sun Sep-May; ⚑; ☐9, 17, ☒A Loop, B Loop, ☒Orange)

FH Steinbart Co
BREWING

4 ⊙ MAP P106, C2

This store offers beer-making classes, along with a great selection of home-brewing equipment. The basic brewing class ($30) is 2½ hours and includes a tasting. There are also regular free demonstrations at the store. Check class schedules online. (☎503-232-8793; www.fhsteinbart.com; 234 SE 12th Ave; classes from $30)

Mazamas
ADVENTURE SPORTS

5 ⊙ MAP P106, G2

Plug into the outdoor-adventure community with courses such as mountaineering, rock climbing and Nordic skiing, run by this educational organization. (☎503-227-2345; www.mazamas.org; 527 SE 43rd Ave; 8-week climbing course $525; ☉office hours 11am-7pm Mon-Thu, 10am-2pm Fri)

Eating

Lardo
SANDWICHES $

6 ✖ MAP P106, C4

Definitely in the running for Portland's best sandwich, Lardo's take on Korean pork shoulder is outstanding – and that's on a menu of a dozen truly fantastic sandwiches. Try a guest-chef creation, different each month, and don't skip the addictive dirty fries, with Parmesan and pork scraps. (📞503-241-2490; www.lardosandwiches.com; 1212 SE Hawthorne Blvd; sandwiches $10-14; 🕐11am-10pm Sun-Thu, to 11pm Fri & Sat; 🚌14)

Nong's Khao Man Gai THAI $

7 MAP P106, B2

The widely adored food cart where it all started has closed, but Nong's brick-and-mortar locations still dish out her signature menu item: tender poached chicken with rice in a magical sauce. A handful of other options (including vegetarian) and add-ons are available, as well as occasional specials. (📞503-740-2907; www.khaomangai.com; 609 SE Ankeny St; mains $11-16; 🕐11am-9pm; 🚌20)

Canard FRENCH $$

8 MAP P106, B2

The hotly anticipated little sibling of chef Gabriel Rucker's rightly famous Le Pigeon (p111), Canard started winning 'best restaurant of the year' designations within weeks of opening at the start of 2018. With its wine-bar-meets-Parisian-brunch-cafe vibe, and a menu of mostly shareable dishes you won't find elsewhere, the place is a champ. (📞971-279-2356; www.canardpdx.com; 734 E Burnside St; dishes $6-20; 🕐8am-midnight Mon-Fri, from 9am Sat & Sun; 🚌20)

Otters at Oaks Bottom Wildlife Refuge

Southeast Eating

Stammtisch

GERMAN $$

9 MAP P106, E1

Dig into serious German food – with a beer list to match – at this dark and cozy neighborhood pub. Don't miss the *Maultaschen* (a pasta pocket filled with leek fondue in a lemony wine sauce), the clams with *Landjäger* sausage in white wine broth, or the paprika-spiced roast chicken. (503-206-7983; www.stammtischpdx. com; 401 NE 28th Ave; small plates $5-9, mains $14-24; 3pm-1:30am Mon-Fri, 11am-1:30am Sat & Sun; 19)

Ken's Artisan Pizza

PIZZA $$

10 MAP P106, E2

Glorious wood-fired, thin-crust pizzas with toppings such as prosciutto, fennel sausage and green garlic. Super-cool atmosphere, with huge sliding windows that open to the street on warm nights. Expect a long wait – no reservations taken. (503-517-9951; www.kensartisan. com; 304 SE 28th Ave; pizzas $13-18; 5-9:30pm Mon-Thu, 5-10pm Fri, 4-10pm Sat, 4-9pm Sun; 20)

Kachka

RUSSIAN $$

11 MAP P106, C3

There's a theme of homey nostalgia at this Russian throwback restaurant, now in a new location and open for lunch as well as dinner. *Babushka*-esque doilies and pastoral Russian artwork accent the experience here, and the food is mostly dumplings and hot or cold *zakuski* (appetizers traditionally washed down with vodka), with a Portland care to keeping ingredients local. (503-235-0059; www.kachkapdx.

Crystal Springs Rhododendron Garden (p108)

JPL DESIGNS/SHUTTERSTOCK ©

com; 960 SE 11th Ave; zakuski $8-14, mains $16-29; ⏰11:30am-2pm & 4-10pm, to 11pm Fri & Sat; 🚌15, 70)

Laurelhurst Market AMERICAN $$$

12 🍴 MAP P106, F2

Hugely popular and vegetarian-unfriendly is this hip and meaty spot, where grass-fed steaks, pork chops and free-range chicken dominate the menu. Just be prepared to wait, unless you have a reservation. There's also a butcher counter selling quality meats and great lunchtime sandwiches. (📞503-206-3097; www.laurelhurstmarket.com; 3155 E Burnside St; mains $17-54; ⏰5-10pm, butcher shop 10am-10pm)

Le Pigeon FRENCH $$$

Squeeze into this cozy, low-lit space next door to sister restaurant Canard (see 8 🍴 Map p106, B2) for some of Portland's best and most-loved cooking. Chef Gabriel Rucker does amazing things with meat and fish and whatever local produce is in season. The seven-course tasting menu ($105) is a complete experience. Sit at the bar to watch the action; most nights there'll be a wait for a table. (📞503-546-8796; www.lepigeon.com; 738 E Burnside St; mains $17-39; ⏰5-10pm; 🚌20)

Drinking

Push x Pull COFFEE

13 ☕ MAP P106, B2

A labor of love by a group of java-obsessed pals, this roastery and cafe specializes in natural-process coffees and offers a rotating selection of single-origins, plus local baked goods. Bright wood paneling and turquoise-painted walls that perfectly match the industrial schoolhouse furniture and espresso machines make for a cheery space – not to mention the delightfully friendly owners and staff. (www.pushxpullcoffee.com; 821 SE Stark St; ⏰7am-5pm Mon-Fri, 8am-4pm Sat & Sun)

Culmination Brewing MICROBREWERY

14 🍺 MAP P106, D1

At this comfortable tasting room in a refurbished old warehouse, you'll find some of the city's best beers (including the top-notch Phaedrus IPA plus a whole array of limited-edition seasonals) and a brief but unusually ambitious food menu. If the *pêche* is available, try it – even if you don't normally like 'fruit' beers. (📞971-254-9114; www.culminationbrewing.com; 2117 NE Oregon St; plates $5-16; ⏰noon-9pm Sun-Thu, to 10pm Fri & Sat; 🚌12)

Scotch Lodge COCKTAIL BAR

15 🍺 MAP P106, B2

Pouring some 300 international and domestic whiskeys in a cozy, subterranean space, Scotch Lodge certainly caters to connoisseurs – but its cocktails that blend whiskey with other spirits are creative and accessible, satisfying aficionado and noob alike. Try the 'Moneypenny' with dry gin, smoky Scotch and sea-bean-infused vermouth. Modern French-inspired bar bites like pumpernickel-battered fried Brie sticks are also available. (📞503-208-2039; www.scotchlodge. com; 215 SE 9th Ave; 🕑4pm-midnight Wed-Sun)

Cider Riot
BREWERY

16 🚇 MAP P106, B2

Portland's best cider company now has its very own pub and tasting room, so you can sample Everybody Pogo, Never Give an Inch or Plastic Paddy at the source. Ciders here are dry and complex, made with regional apples and hyper-regional attitude. (📞503-662-8275; www. ciderriot.com; 807 NE Couch St; 🕑4-11pm Mon-Fri, noon-11pm Sat, noon-9pm Sun; 🚌12, 19, 20)

Migration Brewing
BREWERY

17 🚇 MAP P106, E1

Migration is a popular neighborhood brewpub with a great casual-industrial atmosphere. Wood picnic tables outside make it easy to see and be seen, and are especially wonderful on a warm day. There's good food, and sports fans will appreciate a Blazers or Timbers game on the screens inside. (📞503-206-5221; www.migrationbrewing. com; 2828 NE Glisan St; 🕑11am-11pm Mon-Sat, to 10pm Sun)

Cascade Brewing Barrel House
BREWERY

18 🚇 MAP P106, B3

This excellent brewery special-izes in sour beers, many made from fruit – trust us and give it a

try. If you're hesitant, order a few samplers (or just get the honey-ginger-lime). It all goes well with the gourmet food in the nice, big patio. (📞503-265-8603; www. cascadebrewingbarrelhouse.com; 939 SE Belmont St; 🕑noon-10pm Sun & Mon, to 11pm Tue-Thu, to midnight Fri & Sat)

Hair of the Dog Brewing
BREWERY

19 🚇 MAP P106, A3

HOTD brews unusual beer styles, some of which are 'bottle-conditioned,' whereby the brewing cycle is finished inside the bottle. This results in complex flavors and high alcohol content, and the beer ages like a fine wine. Food is served to complement the beer's flavors. (📞503-232-6585; www.hairofthedog. com; 61 SE Yamhill St; 🕑11:30am-10pm Tue-Sat, to 8pm Sun; 🚌4, 6, 10, 14, 15, 🚋A Loop)

Hopworks Urban Brewery
BREWERY

20 🚇 MAP P106, E6

All-organic beers made with local ingredients and served in an ecofriendly building with bicycle frames above the bar. Try the IPA or the Survival Stout, made with Stumptown coffee. There's a good selection of food and a family-friendly atmosphere, and the back deck can't be beat on a warm day. (HUB; 📞503-232-4677; www.hopworksbeer.com; 2944 SE Powell Blvd; 🕑11am-11pm Sun-Thu, to midnight Fri & Sat; 👶; 🚌9)

Horse Brass Pub

PUB

 21 MAP P106, H3

Portland's most established English pub, cherished for its dark-wood atmosphere, excellent fish-and-chips and nearly 60 beers on tap. Also serves 'proper' 20oz imperial pints. Play some darts, watch soccer on TV and reminisce about the days when you couldn't see across the room through all the smoke. (📞503-232-2202; www.horsebrass.com; 4534 SE Belmont St; ⏱11am-2:30am)

Crush

GAY

22 MAP P106, C3

Slip into this sexy lounge with all the pretty people, order one of the exotic cocktails and speak up – it gets loud, what with all the dancing and shows. Everyone is friendly and welcoming no matter what your leanings may be, and the cocktails and bar snacks are top-notch. (📞503-235-8150; www.crushbar.com; 1400 SE Morrison St; ⏱noon-2am, from 10am Sat & Sun)

Hey Love

COCKTAIL BAR

23 MAP P106, B2

Bright, colorful, high-octane craft cocktails and boozy, fruity frozen concoctions elicit perpetual summer vibes at this women-led lounge, attached to the Jupiter Next hotel. Rattan light fixtures, antique Moroccan carpets, thrift-store art and knick-knacks, and living plants suspended from the ceiling create a cozily eclectic atmosphere. A full menu of

Cascade Brewing Barrel House

internationally inspired dishes is served for lunch and dinner, plus weekend brunch. (📞503-206-6223; www.heylovepdx.com; 920 E Burnside St; 🕐7am-2am)

Entertainment

Laurelhurst Theater
CINEMA

24 ⭐ MAP P106, E2

This great neighborhood theater has moved from showing second-run to mostly first-run movies, with occasional revival series. Pizza, salads, beer and wine are available; kids are welcome (with a parent) before 8pm. On Tuesday all tickets are matinee price. (📞503-232-5511; www.laurelhursttheater.com; 2735 E Burnside St; tickets $6.50-9; 🚃20)

Bagdad Theater
CINEMA

25 ⭐ MAP P106, F4

This awesome, historic McMenamins venue offers microbrews on tap and pizza, burgers, salads and bar grub to go with its first-run films. (📞503-236-9234; www.bagdadmovies.com; 3702 SE Hawthorne Blvd; adult/child under 12yr $10/7)

Doug Fir Lounge
LIVE MUSIC

26 ⭐ MAP P106, B2

Combining futuristic elements with a rustic log-cabin aesthetic, this venue has helped transform the LoBu (lower Burnside) neighborhood from seedy to slick. Doug Fir books great bands and the sound quality is usually tops. The attached restaurant offers a killer breakfast, weekend brunch and a bar menu ($8 to $13) until close. (📞503-231-9663; www.dougfirlounge.com; 830 E Burnside St; 🕐7am-2:30am; 🚃20)

Goodfoot
LIVE MUSIC

27 ⭐ MAP P106, E2

Very neighborly spot with affordable music acts in the basement, plus good dancing (especially Friday nights) and a great sound system. Upstairs is a bar with booths, cheap pool tables, stiff drinks and creative art on the walls. Check out the open-mike night on Monday. (📞503-239-9292; www.thegoodfoot.com; 2845 SE Stark St)

Revolution Hall
CONCERT VENUE

28 ⭐ MAP P106, C2

Inside a remodeled 1924 school building (whose famous alumni include James Beard and Linus Pauling), this 850-seat concert venue has great sound quality and no bad seats. There's a rooftop bar with views toward downtown Assembly, a bar-lounge with 24 beers on tap; and two ground-floor cafe-bars, Martha's and the new Show Bar. (📞503-288-3895, tickets 877-435-9849; www.revolutionhall.com; 1300 SE Stark St; 🕐box office 5-7pm; 🚃15, 70)

Oaks Park
AMUSEMENT PARK

29 ⭐ MAP P106, C6

This amusement park in the is just run-down enough to be charming and kitschy, with fun rides, go-karts and a roller-skating rink.

The Hangar plays host to the **Rose City Rollers** (www.rosecity rollers.com; tickets from $15) roller derby team, whose showdowns are fast, furious and very entertaining. (📞 503-233-5777; www.oakspark.com; 7805 SE Oaks Park Way)

Hawthorne Theatre   LIVE MUSIC

30 📷 MAP P106, G4

A good-sized, boxy venue inside a former Masonic Lodge, the Hawthorne Theatre is one of the few places in town that has an all-ages section. There's also a lounge that hosts more intimate gigs (21 years and over only). Check the calendar online for upcoming shows. (📞 503-233-7100; www.hawthornetheatre.com; 1507 SE 39th Ave; 🚌 14)

Shopping

ZimZim   GIFTS & SOUVENIRS

31 🏠 MAP P106, E1

An 'alternative' gift shop crammed with saucy birthday cards, badass-woman T-shirts and various other treasures (eg 'dumps for Trump' dog-poop bags, Mr Rogers lapel pins), this little corner store is a fun place to browse. You'll likely find something for that person you can otherwise never find a perfect present for. (📞 503-235-0518; www.zimzimpdx.com; 144 NE 28th Ave; 🕐 11am-7pm Mon-Sat, to 6pm Sun; 🚌 19, 20)

Next Adventure   SPORTS & OUTDOORS

32 🏠 MAP P106, B2

This awesome outdoor store has plenty of sports clothing (including discounted items) and gear for hiking, camping, skiing and whatever else you have in mind. There's also a downstairs 'bargain basement' of used clothing and gear. (📞 503-233-0706; www.nextadventure.net; 426 SE Grand Ave; 🕐 10am-7pm Mon-Fri, to 6pm Sat, 11am-5pm Sun; 🚌 6, 🚋 A Loop, B Loop)

Music Millennium   MUSIC

33 🏠 MAP P106, F2

This place is a revelation with its extensive collections of everything from classic rock to straight-up classical. Check the listings of live in-store performances and grab a 'Keep Portland Weird!' sticker while you're here. (📞 503-231-8926; www.musicmillennium.com; 3158 E Burnside St; 🕐 10am-10pm Mon-Sat, 11am-9pm Sun)

Pairings   WINE

34 🏠 MAP P106, D1

This quirky wine shop pairs its products with rock songs, astrological signs and various moods (as well as more conventional food pairings). Most of the wines it sells are made from organically grown grapes. There are frequent classes and special events; check the website for details. (📞 541-531-7653; www.pairingsportland.com; 455 NE 24th Ave; 🕐 noon-10pm Mon-Sat, to 7pm Sun; 🚌 12, 19, 20)

Worth a Trip 🔭
Discover Columbia River Gorge

Driving east from Portland on I-84 (or on the scenic Historic Columbia River Hwy) has you passing high waterfalls and nearly vertical mountain walls that parallel the mighty Columbia. Hiking trails lead through fern-lined canyons and gushing rivers to grand vistas while wind sports, mountain biking and rafting opportunities abound. Wash the adventure down with wine, beer and cider tasting.

🚌 The Columbia Gorge Express service from Northeast Portland (Gateway) to Multnomah Falls ($2.50), Cascade Locks ($5) and Hood River ($7.50) allows you to visit the gorge for the day from Portland, without driving.

Columbia River Highway

Finished in 1915, the Historic Columbia River Hwy winds its scenic way between Troutdale and the Dalles. Also known as Hwy 30, the route offers access to waterfalls and awe-inspiring views all year round. Hwy 84 runs parallel and offers a much faster but less scenic route through the Columbia River Gorge.

From Portland, once you've passed Troutdale and entered the scenic area, you'll first come to a few viewpoints including the lovely (and often windy) **Vista House** (pictured; ☏503-344-1368; www.vistahouse.com; admission free; ⏱9am-4pm Oct-Apr, to 6pm May-Sep). The drive from here brings you to impressive waterfall after waterfall along the mossy, evergreen-clad roadside.

The tiny blue-collar town of Cascade Locks (at exit 44 off I-84; 44 miles from Portland) sits pretty on the Columbia River and you can visit the massive **Bonneville Dam** (☏541-374-8820; admission free; ⏱9am-5pm) nearby as well as Herman the (gigantic) sturgeon at the **Bonneville Fish Hatchery** (☏541-374-8393; 70543 NE Herman Loop; admission free; ⏱7am-5pm Nov-Feb, to 8pm Mar-Oct).

Hood River

The dynamic, gentrified town of Hood River (63 miles from Portland) is one of the best windsurfing and kiteboarding destinations in the world and attracts photogenic enthusiasts who zip back and forth across the wide Columbia River.

But Hood River offers more than awesome winds. The city has a bustling and pretty commercial core, with excellent shops, bars and restaurants lining a few steeply angled streets. In summer fruit stands and U-picks sell apples, pears, cherries, berries and vegetables. Premier wineries, breweries and cideries have also taken strong hold in the region.

★ Top Tips

o The best views of the gorge are from Portland Women's Forum Park and Vista House.

o Arrive before 9:30am to get parking at Multnomah Falls on weekends and sunny days.

✕ Take a Break

Eat at a Hood River brewery like **Ferment Brewing Company** (☏541-436-3499; www.fermentbrewing. com; 403 Portway Ave; beer/kombucha flights $10/7; ⏱11am-9pm Sun-Thu, to 10pm Fri & Sat).

For family-friendly grub on the riverside, don't miss **Thunder Island Brewing Co** (☏971-231-4599; www. thunderislandbrewing. com; 515 NW Portage Rd; mains $10-17, flights from $8; ⏱noon-8pm Mon-Wed, 11am-9pm Fri-Sun; 👫👶) in Cascade Locks.

Pick up some local smoked salmon for the road from Native American vendors under the Bridge of the Gods.

Consider taking a windsurfing or kiteboarding lesson – **Big Winds** (☎888-509-4210; www.bigwinds.com; 207 Front St; lessons $49; ⏱9am-5pm) is the biggest operator and is in downtown Hood River. It rents stand-up paddleboards too. Head south of town for great mountain biking. Most of the area's trails are off Hwy 35 and Forest Rd 44 (which branches off Hwy 35 about 20 miles south of Hood River). Good local rides include Post Canyon, Surveyor's Ridge and Nestor Peak. You can rent bikes at **Discover Bicycles** (☎541-386-4820; www.discoverbicycles.com; 210 State St; rentals per day $40-100; ⏱10am-6pm Mon-Sat, to 5pm Sun).

The Fruit Loop to Mt Hood

Covering 35 miles up Hwy 35, along scenic fertile lands and up a flank of Mt Hood, the Hood River County Fruit Loop takes you by family fruit stands, U-pick orchards, lavender fields, alpaca farms and winery tasting rooms. There are blossoms in spring, berries in summer, and apples and pears in fall – with plenty of festivals and celebrations throughout the seasons (except for winter). It's a good way to sample the area's agricultural bounties while appreciating the local scenery too. Backtrack to Portland through the Gorge or drive over Mt Hood to Hwy 26 to add another hour to your drive. For more

Top Waterfalls

Waterfalls are at their gushiest in spring. The following are all off Hwy 30 (the Historic Columbia River Hwy), listed from west to east.

Bridal Veil Falls (140ft) Two-tiered falls reached via an easy half-mile walk. A separate wheelchair-accessible trail leads to great views.

Wahkeena Falls (242ft) Hike up the Wahkeena Trail, join Trail No 441 and head down to Multnomah Falls. Return via the road for the 4.8-mile loop.

Multnomah Falls (620ft) The gorge's top attraction. A 1-mile trail leads to the top. Continue up forested Multnomah Creek and the top of Larch Mountain (another 7 miles).

Horsetail Falls (176ft) Just east of Oneonta Gorge. A 2.6-mile loop begins here, passing through Ponytail Falls (and with an optional side trail to Triple Falls). Walk a half-mile east on Hwy 30 (passing the Oneonta Gorge) to return.

information and a list of events, check www.hoodriverfruitloop.com.

Easter Gorge & the Dalles

Located about 85 miles east of Portland, the Dalles features a decidedly different climate – much drier and sunnier. Though steadfastly unglamorous and down to earth (except for a few historic buildings), the city offers good outdoor recreation; there's decent camping and hiking, and fierce winds that are excellent for windsurfing and kiteboarding. The major stop here is the fun and educational **Columbia Gorge Discovery Center** (📞541-296-8600; www.gorgediscovery.org; 5000 Discovery Dr; adult/child $9/5; ⏱9am-5pm) that covers the area's history from the floods that carved it to the Lewis and Clark expedition. For something a little more offbeat,

the new **National Neon Sign Museum** (📞541-370-2242; www.nationalneonsignmuseum.org; 20 East 3rd St; ⏱10am-5pm Thu-Sat, reduced hours in winter; 👶) teaches you all about light bulbs and neon tubes.

East of The Dalles, the sights thin out a bit, and the landscapes turn from lush and mossy to windswept golden grass. It's a long drive to anywhere but there are some worthy places to check out, including the remarkable **Maryhill Museum of Art** (📞509-773-3733; www.maryhillmuseum.org; 35 Maryhill Museum Dr; adult/child $12/5; ⏱10am-5pm mid-Mar–mid-Nov) and a replica of **Stonehenge** (US Hwy 97; admission free). Wine lovers should hit the brakes at **Maryhill Winery** (📞877-627-9445; www.maryhillwinery.com; 9774 Hwy 14; ⏱noon-8pm Mon-Thu, to 9pm Fri & Sat, to 7pm Sun).

Willamette Valley Regions

Forest Grove

 Portland

McMinnville (p123)
The classic Americana downtown here is a great place to shop country-chic shops, dine and base yourself for a wine country adventure.

Gaston

Newberg & Dundee (p133)
You'll find some exceptional dining and luxurious lodging in these small towns, that all pair great with tasting pinot noir at nearby wineries.

Salem (p141)
Visit the state capitol then head to nearby hot springs, a waterfall-filled state park and a Bavarian town topped with a Benedictine monastery.

Woodburn

Monmouth

Explore the Willamette Valley

The Willamette Valley is world famous for its fabulous and plentiful wineries, which could easily take several days to explore. They're not the region's only highlight, however. Visit humble Salem, Oregon's capital city, for its museums and stately buildings. Everything is so close by you'll want to linger for longer than you planned, so stretch that schedule and put on your explorer's hat – you'll need it.

Explore McMinnville

At the heart of the region's wine industry lies busy and modern McMinnville, mostly charmless except for its historic, redbrick downtown district. Here you'll find art galleries, boutiques, wine-tasting rooms, fine restaurants and a few good hotels. The main regional attractions are the area's wineries, of course – many people opt to base themselves in McMinnville or nearby in order to explore the region.

The Short List

○ **Wineries (p124)** *Learning about the complexities of pinot noir in lovely, laid-back tasting rooms.*

○ **Dining (p130)** *Sampling the exceptional locally driven menus at some of the most sought-after tables in the state.*

○ **Downtown McMinnville** *Browsing scenic downtown's architecture, art galleries and adorable shops.*

○ **Evergreen Aviation & Space Museum (p128)** *Getting geeky about airplanes then watersliding your cares away at the water park next door.*

○ **Festivals** *Seeing the valley at its most lively during festivals like the International Pinot Noir Celebration and Wine Country Thanksgiving.*

Getting There & Around

🚗 Renting a car is your best transport option. For chauffeured winery tours, check with the Chamber of Commerce.

🚌 Yamhill County Transit Area provides bus service around Yamhill County, with connections to Portland's MAX light-rail system and Salem.

McMinnville Map on p126

Grapes in the Willamette Valley JENNIFER LARSEN MORROW/SHUTTERSTOCK ©

Top Experience 📷
Taste Fine Wines in the Willamette Valley

🚗 Designate a sober driver or hire a guide.

Often considered the heart of the wine country, McMinnville and the surrounding areas are where the bulk of the Willamette Valley's wineries are located. Carlton, 7 miles north of McMinnville, and Dayton, 7 miles east, feature several vineyards, tasting rooms and retreats for oenophiles thirsty to sample Oregon's finest wines.

Oregon's Wine Bounty

Oregon's first wineries started up in the 1850s, but it wasn't until the late 1960s and early 1970s that the region's winemaking potential started to bear fruit. The northern Willamette Valley's mild climate and long summers foster the delicate pinot noir grape, as well as pinot gris, chardonnay and riesling.

Most vineyards are family-owned and welcome visitors to their tasting rooms, which range from grand edifices to homey affairs tucked into the corner of fermentation rooms. Before heading out to the wineries, double-check tasting-room hours (usually noon to 5pm Wednesday to Sunday, but some are open daily) and tasting fees ($10 to $20 for a flight).

Get a winery map at McMinnville's Chamber of Commerce, or see www.willamettewines. com, as there are more than 500 wineries in the region, and you'll want to narrow it down to two or three in a day. If the weather's nice, pack a lunch; wineries usually can't offer food, but many have picnic grounds.

If you're short of time, you don't have to visit the wineries to sip local wines. Some of the bigger wineries have tasting rooms in downtown Newberg, Dundee, Carlton or McMinnville. And there are always the region's restaurants, with their excellent wine lists.

Celebrate Grapes

Held in late July, the **International Pinot Noir Celebration** (www.ipnc.org; one-day pass $150; ☉Jul) is an important testing ground for pinot noir wines from all over the world. The three-day festival is immensely popular despite costing $1295 per person (including some meals); there's a public tasting on Sunday.

Wineries all across the Willamette Valley celebrate the **Thanksgiving holiday** (www. willamettewines.com; ☉Nov) with a weekend of special tastings, live music, food, tours and various other events.

★ **Top Tips**

o Pop into the **Chamber of Commerce** (☎503-472-6196; www. mcminnville.org; 417 NW Adams St; ☉8am-5pm Mon-Fri) in McMinnville for maps, tips and information on wineries and other attractions in the area before you head out.

o For the most relaxing approach, have a local tour operator drive you around. Good local choices include **Grape Escape** (☎503-283-3380; www.grapeescapetours. com; tours from $125), Oregon Select Wine Tours (p136) and Valley Vineyard Tours (p136).

✕ **Take a Break**

There's good eating in McMinnville, including some of the most sought-after tables in the state. Be sure to book ahead if you have your heart set on something.

For a break from all that wine, have a beer with lunch at Golden Valley Brewery (p130).

A B C D

Carlton ⊗ 12

1

NE 9th St
NE Davis St
NE 8th St
NE Ford St
NE 7th St
NE Galloway St
NE 10th Ave
7 ⊙ Eyrie Vineyards
NE Alpine Ave
NE 9th Ave
NE 7th Ave
N Lafayette Ave

2

NE 6th St
NE Evans St
NE 5th St
NE Ford St
NE Galloway St
NE 4th St
NE Irvine St
N Johnson St
NE Kirby St
NE Logan St

14 ⊗
NE 3rd St
⊗ 15
⊗ 13
5 ⊙
Anne Amie Vineyards

⊗ 11
17
NE 2nd St

0   200 m
0   0.1 miles

McMinnville

3

47

4

99W

5

See McMinnville
Enlargement

Yamhill River

McMinnville ⊙

6

Evergreen Wings &
Waves Waterpark
9 ⊙
1 ⊙ Evergreen Aviation
& Space Museum

A B C D

For reviews see

⊙ Sights	p128
✗ Eating	p130

1

0 ——————— 2 km
0 ——————— 1 miles

2

Milican Creek

Domaine
Serene
8 ⊙

⊙ 3
Domaine
Drouhin

White Rose ⊙ 4
Estate

10 ⊙
Equestrian
Wine Tours

3

McMinnville

Remy
Wines
2 ⊙

99W

● Lafayette

6 ⊙
Stoller Family
Estate

4

233

Yamhill River

233

Yamhill
Locks
Park

● Dayton

5

Willamette River

✗ 16

18

6

233

E   F   G   H

Sights

Evergreen Aviation & Space Museum

MUSEUM

1 ◉ MAP P126, D6

A mile east of McMinnville, this museum showcases Howard Hughes' *Spruce Goose,* the world's largest wood-framed airplane. In 1947, with Hughes at the wheel, the airplane flew for just under a mile – and never took off again. Plenty of other aircraft are on display, including propeller planes, small jets, fighters, biplanes and helicopters. A different building offers excellent space-exploration exhibits. There's also a 3-D digital theater, along with two cafes and gift shops. Tours are available. (📞503-434-4180; www.evergreenmuseum.org; 500 NE Captain Michael King Smith Way; adult/child $19/27; ⏱9am-5pm; 🚼)

Remy Wines

WINE

2 ◉ MAP P126, G4

In a landscape known for French heritage wines, Remy Drabkin brings old world Italy to the Willamette Valley. Specializing in single-vineyard, single-varietal Italian wines, Remy's craft isn't the only unique thing about her – she could be the only Jewish lesbian winemaker in Oregon. Sip sangiovese or dolcetto at the rustic tasting room set in a historic farmhouse in the Dundee foothills. (📞503-864-8777; www.remywines.com; 17495 NE McDougall Rd; flights $10-15; ⏱noon-5pm)

Domaine Drouhin

WINE

3 ◉ MAP P126, H3

For grand atmosphere and panoramic views, plus well-established pinot and chardonnay from the surrounding Dundee Hills, stop in at Domaine Drouhin. (📞503-864-2700; www.domainedrouhin.com; 6750 NE Breymen Orchards Rd; flights $20; ⏱11am-4pm)

White Rose Estate

WINE

4 ◉ MAP P126, G3

Set atop a hill with sweeping views of surrounding vineyards, White Rose is heralded for pinot noirs made in a 'neoclassical' style – a modern approach to historical, whole-cluster fermentation. Built into the hill and over the cellar, the chilly, windowless tasting room still manages to elicit an inviting warmth, thanks in large part to the cheery and knowledgeable manager, Dago Guillén. (📞503-864-2328; www.whiteroseestate.com; 6250 NE Hilltop Lane; tastings $25; ⏱11am-5pm)

Anne Amie Vineyards

WINE

5 ◉ MAP P126, D3

You'll find some very distinctive pinot noirs and zero pretentiousness at this fun and friendly tasting room located just outside Carlton. The reserve pinot noir and sparkling rosé are top notch, and for those after something a little different there's also a dessert wine on offer. (📞503-864-2991; www.anneamie.com; 6580 NE Mineral

Springs Rd; flights $15; ⏱10am-4:45pm daily Mar-Dec, Thu-Mon only Jan & Feb)

Stoller Family Estate WINE

6 ⊚ MAP P126, G4

The world's first LEED Gold–certified winery, Stoller is as impressive as it is easy to reach. The 4000-sq-ft tasting room is well worth checking out, even for non-enthusiasts. (⏰503-864-3404; www.stollerfamilyestate.com; 16161 NE McDougall Rd; flights $20; ⏱11am-5pm)

Eyrie Vineyards WINE

7 ⊚ MAP P126, C1

Eyrie is home to the first pinot noir and chardonnay plantings in the Willamette Valley, and the first pinot gris plantings in the US. Find the remodeled tasting room in McMinnville, open by appointment Thursday through Monday, with seatings at 11am and 2pm. (⏰503-472-6315; www.eyrievineyards.com; 935 NE 10th Ave; tastings $40; ⏱tastings by appointment only, 11am & 2pm Thu-Mon)

Domaine Serene WINE

8 ⊚ MAP P126, G2

Try the rosé or the signature pinot noirs amid stunning views at this hilltop vineyard. (⏰503-864-4600; www.domaineserene.com; 6555 NE Hilltop Lane; tasting fee $25; ⏱tasting room 11am-4pm Mon-Thu, to 5pm Fri-Sun)

McMinnville Sights

Evergreen Aviation & Space Museum

RITU MANOJ JETHANI/SHUTTERSTOCK ©

Evergreen Wings & Waves Waterpark
WATER PARK

9 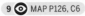 MAP P126, C6

A must on a hot day, this indoor water park is next to the aviation museum (p128) and quite unmissable – a retired Boeing 747 lies atop the building. Inside are 10 waterslides (including four that come out of the 747), a wave pool, a splashing play structure, a leisure pool and a bubbly toddler area. Plenty of lifeguards keep everyone safe. (📞503-687-3390; https://wingsandwaveswaterpark.com; 500 NE Captain Michael King Smith Way; visitors under/over 42in $20/29, dry passes $10; ⏰10am-6pm or 7pm, varies with season; 🚼)

Equestrian Wine Tours
WINE

10 🔘 MAP P126, E3

Tour the Red Hills around Dundee on horseback or by carriage, stopping at various winery tasting rooms. Minimal risk of a DUI! Tours depart from Winter's Hill Estate (www.wintershillwine.com) in Dayton. (📞503-864-2336; www.equestrianwinetours.com; 6325 NE Abbey Rd; 2.5hr tour per person $190)

Eating

Crescent Cafe
AMERICAN $$

11 🍴 MAP P126, B3

Solid breakfast spot serving up comfort dishes like creamed chicken and biscuits with eggs, or a grilled ham and cheddar sandwich with caramelized onions. Try the passion-fruit bellini and apple cinnamon crepes or a classic Reuben sandwich for lunch. Expect a long wait on weekends. (📞503-435-2655; www.crescentcafeonthird.com; 526 NE 3rd St; breakfast mains $6-14; ⏰7am-2pm Wed-Fri, from 8am Sat & Sun)

The Horse Radish
AMERICAN $$

12 🍴 MAP P126, B1

Gourmet meals, cheese plates and a wine bar in the heart of Carlton, with weekly dinner specials (6pm to 8pm Friday and Saturday) featuring dishes like BBQ shrimp and cheddar grits, or green chili-stuffed chicken breasts with black beans and rice. There's live music on Friday and Saturday nights. (📞503-852-6656; www.thehorseradish.com; 211 W Main St; small-plate combos $12-18; ⏰noon-3pm Sun-Thu, to 10pm Fri & Sat)

Golden Valley Brewery
AMERICAN $$

13 🍴 MAP P126, C3

This top-notch brewery-restaurant offers great small plates, salads and sandwiches, along with gourmet burgers and steaks – made with meat from its own ranch. (📞503-472-2739; www.goldenvalleybrewery.com; 980 NE 4th St; mains $9-25; ⏰11am-10pm Mon-Thu, to 11pm Fri & Sat, to 9pm Sun)

Nick's Italian Cafe ITALIAN $$

14 🗙 MAP P126, B3

Going strong for over 30 years, Nick's was named one of 'America's Classics' by the James Beard Foundation in 2014. It doesn't offer slick, contemporary decor, but it does have timeless Italian cuisine. There's also excellent wood-fired pizza and great appetizers. (📞503-434-4471; www.nicksitaliancafe.com; 521 NE 3rd St; pizzas $15-17, mains $16-29; 🕔5-9pm Thu-Tue)

Bistro Maison FRENCH $$$

15 🗙 MAP P126, B3

This European eatery is one of McMinnville's, and the region's, best restaurants, serving up exceptional French dishes like duck confit, *cassoulet* (casserole with meat and white beans) and *coq au vin* (chicken braised in red wine). Try the croque monsieur or madame for lunch (mains $14 to $19). The lovely garden patio is mandatory on warm summer nights. (📞503-474-1888; www.bistromaison.com; 729 NE 3rd St; mains $28-38; 🕔5:30-9pm Wed-Sat, noon-7pm Sun)

Joel Palmer House NORTHWESTERN US $$$

16 🗙 MAP P126, G5

Renowned for its dishes built around wild mushrooms and Oregon truffles (often handpicked by the chef, Christopher Czarnecki), this highly lauded restaurant is just a few miles northwest of McMinnville, in Dayton. It's one of Oregon's finest eateries, turning local ingredients into unforgettable fine cuisine. Reservations recommended. (📞503-864-2995; www.joelpalmerhouse.com; 600 Ferry St; 3-course menu from $65; 🕔4:30-9:30pm Tue-Sat)

Thistle NORTHWESTERN US $$$

17 🗙 MAP P126, B3

Small but top-drawer restaurant run by Eric Bechard, an award-winning chef who fiercely believes in using local, organic ingredients whenever possible. The menu changes daily and is posted on a chalkboard, and while portions are small they are well created and truly delicious. If you're having decision fatigue after a long day, your table can opt for the 'Chef's Whim.' (📞503-472-9623; www.thistlerestaurant.com; 228 NE Evans St; mains $24-27; 🕔5:30-9pm Tue-Sat)

Explore ◈
Newberg & Dundee

The gateways to wine country, these small cities, just a couple of miles apart, were originally founded as Quaker settlements. These days, car traffic, strip malls and modern services are much of what you'll see. There are excellent restaurants here, however, along with upscale places to sleep.

The Short List

○ **Wine tasting (p136)** *Sampling the best pinots of the region at wineries and tasting rooms spread in and around these towns.*

○ **Champoeg State Heritage Area (p137)** *Taking a break from wine to explore serene woodlands and riverbanks and learn about Oregon history.*

○ **Dining (p137)** *Delighting in the good food around here, from picnic supplies to fine dining.*

○ **Shopping (p139)** *Heading into an adorable shop like Velour to go vintage Pacific Northwest to handmade country-chic.*

Getting There & Around

Dundee is 2 miles west of Newberg, on Hwy 99W.

🚗 Renting a car is the best way to get around. Numerous wine tours are also available.

🚌 Caravan Shuttle provides shuttle services to/from Portland's airport ($42 one-way per person).

Newberg & Dundee Map on p134

Champoeg State Heritage Area (p137) SHANE N. COTEE/SHUTTERSTOCK ©

For reviews see

👁	Sights	p136
✗	Eating	p137
🔒	Shopping	p139

0 ————— 1 km
0 ————— 0.5 miles

99W

9 ✗

Newberg

See Newberg
Enlargment

219

18

Newberg

E Sheridan St

George Fox
University

N Blaine St

N Howard St

E Hancock St

N College St

N Edwards St

N Meridian St

N Center St

N River St

E 1st St

N Hwy 99W

Chehalem

✗ 👁 ✗
7 13 8

👁 3

Hoover
Park

Hoover-Minthorn
House 1 👁

6 ✗

S Blaine St

S Howard St

E 2nd St

11 ✗

S College St

S Edwards St

S Meridian St

S Center St

S River St

E 3rd St

0 ————— 200 m
0 ————— 0.1 miles

Sights

Hoover-Minthorn House
MUSEUM

1 ⊙ MAP P134, H5

This house is where Herbert Hoover (the 31st president of the USA) grew up. Built in 1881, the restored home is now a museum of period furnishings and early Oregon history. Call ahead outside summer; hours vary, but appointments are possible during off season. (☎503-538-6629; www.hooverminthorn.org; 115 S River St; adult/child $5/free; ⏰1-4pm Wed-Sun Mar-Oct, closed Jan, limited hours rest of year)

ROCO Winery
WINE

2 ⊙ MAP P134, C1

Named after its delightful owners, Rollin and Corby Soles, ROCO specializes in small-production pinot noir, chardonnay and sparkling wines. Rollin, co-founder and former head winemaker at **Argyle Winery** (☎503-538-8520; www.argylewinery.com; 691 Hwy 99W; flights $20; ⏰11am-5pm Mon-Thu, from 10am Fri-Sun), has been a pioneer of Oregon sparkling wine for more than 30 years. The 2016 RMS Brut Rosé is a particular standout, best enjoyed on the cozy tasting room's zen-garden patio. (☎503-538-7625; www.rocowinery.com; 13260 NE Red Hills Rd; tasting flights $15-20; ⏰11am-5pm)

Oregon Select Wine Tours
WINE

Focusing on boutique wineries around Newberg, Dundee and McMinnville, Oregon Select Wine Tours provides custom tours in full-size luxury SUVs. The hourly rate is for up to six people; ask about larger groups. Add a gourmet picnic lunch or charcuterie plate for an additional fee. (☎971-404-5178; www.oregonselectwinetours.com; tour per hour $75)

Valley Vineyard Tours
WINE

This Newberg-based operation provides laid-back, custom wine country tours for up to six passengers ($100 per hour for more than six). Can also arrange airport transfers to and from Newberg ($110). (☎971-267-5444; www.valleyvineyardtours.com; tour per hour $75)

Chehalem
WINE

3 ⊙ MAP P134, H5

Private tastings at the winery; public tastings at its Newberg tasting room. There's also wine on tap at the tasting room, where you can fill up a keepsake glass bottle. (☎503-538-4700; www.chehalemwines.com; 106 S Center St; flights $20; ⏰11am-5pm Sun-Thu, to 8pm Fri & Sat)

Lange Estate Winery & Vineyards
WINE

4 ⊙ MAP P134, A3

Family-run Lange is known for good-value, single-vineyard pinot noir. The grounds have gorgeous views and shaggy dogs running around. (📞 503-538-6476; www.langewinery.com; 18380 NE Buena Vista Dr; tastings from $15; 🕙 11am-5pm)

Eating

Red Hills Market   AMERICAN $

5 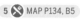 MAP P134, B5

This deli-market offers a great atmosphere, with its wines and gourmet food products surrounding a small cluster of diners in the main room. Head to the excellent back patio to enjoy your toasted, open-faced 'craft' sandwich, made from fancy charcuterie, or a (semi) healthy breakfast bowl. A few salads and wood-fired pizzas are also available. (📞 971-832-8414; www. redhillsmarket.com; 155 SW 7th St; mains $7-18; 🕙 7am-8pm)

Storrs Smokehouse   BARBECUE $

6 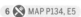 MAP P134, E5

The folks behind the upscale Painted Lady (p138) have taken their genius down home with this Southern-style barbecue joint. Brisket, pulled pork, ribs and wings are smoked for days, resulting in slip-off-the-bone tenderness and deep flavor. Can't pick a protein? Try them all with the Grandaddy platter. Slather everything in their homemade Oregon Pinot Noir BBQ sauce. Let meat coma ensue. (📞 503-538-8080; www.storrssmokehouse.com; 310 E 1st St; meat plates $8-19; 🕙 8am-8pm Wed-Sun)

Champoeg State Heritage Area

A state heritage area and popular family destination, **Champoeg** (📞 503-678-1251; www.oregonstateparks.org; 7679 Champoeg Rd NE; day fee $5; 🕙 10am-4:30pm; 🚼) is 25 miles southwest of Portland and 6 miles southeast of Newberg. There are 615 acres of old-growth woodland, grassy meadows, nature trails, historic sites, campgrounds and a playground. Films and displays at the visitor center explain the events that led up to the famous vote, in 1843, that formed the Northwest's first provisional government.

Rosmarino Osteria Italiana   ITALIAN $$

7 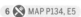 MAP P134, G5

Originally from outside of Milan, chef Dario Pisoni prepares simple and delicious northern Italian dishes based on recipes inherited from his *nonna* (grandmother). Key ingredients like olive oil, cheese, flour and Carnaroli rice are all imported from his native home, and you can expect classics like hearty braised meats and risotto on the weekly changing menu. Reservations essential. (📞 503-438-6211; www.osteriarosmarino.com; 714 E 1st St; lunch mains $8-15, five-course tasting menu $95; 🕙 11:30am-2:30pm & 5:30-8pm Thu, 11:30am-2:30pm &

6:30-8pm Fri, 11:30am-2:30pm & 6:30-9pm Sat, 11:30am-7:30pm Sun & Mon)

Ruddick/Wood
AMERICAN $$

8 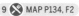 MAP P134, G5

Set in a converted 1920s garage, this classy yet casual restaurant and tavern has perfected local, seasonal new-American fare. The open kitchen, encircled by a copper-top bar with seating, cranks out small plates like duck and oat hushpuppies and crispy Dungeness crab and shrimp cakes. Heartier mains include chicken roulade and mushroom and shell bean falafel with cauliflower couscous. (☎503-487-6133; www.ruddickwood.com; 720 E 1st St; dinner mains $13-28; ⏱11:30am-10:30pm Tue-Thu, to 11:30pm Fri, 10am-11:30pm Sat, 10am-10:30pm Sun)

Newbergundian Bistro
BISTRO $$

9 MAP P134, F2

This cozy bistro with an open kitchen serves up American classics like burgers, a wedge salad and oysters Rockefeller, plus European-inspired fare. Bouillabaisse with shrimp, mussels and halibut, crispy polenta with hazelnut pesto, and a croque monsieur with smoked ham hock are all expertly executed. The service is swift and cheery. (☎971-832-8687; www.newbergundian.com; 203 Villa Rd; dinner mains $11-26; ⏱11am-10pm Mon, Wed, Thu & Sun, to 11pm Fri & Sat)

Dundee Bistro
NORTHWESTERN US $$

10 MAP P134, B5

This modern, popular restaurant is owned by Ponzi Vineyards and has a wine-tasting room next door. Dishes like Oregon Ling cod and chips, or pappardelle pasta with braised wild boar grace the menu, which changes seasonally. The gourmet pizza offers a more casual option. On warm days go for the great back patio. (☎503-554-1650; www.dundeebistro.com; 100 SW 7th St; mains $16-32; ⏱11:30am-9pm)

Painted Lady
NORTHWESTERN US $$$

11 MAP P134, F5

Accomplished chefs Allen Routt and Jessica Bagley use their wide travel and culinary experiences at this renowned restaurant in a renovated 1890s Victorian house. The multicourse set menus include choices of appetizer, like Dungeness crab with miso custard, mains like dry-aged New York strip steaks with pea puree, and desserts like honey lavender mousse, with the option of a wine pairing. (☎503-538-3850; www.thepaintedladyrestaurant.com; 201 S College St; prix fixe $95-110; ⏱5-10pm Wed-Sun)

Tina's
NORTHWESTERN US $$$

12 MAP P134, B6

This small, renowned French-influenced restaurant does meat

dishes such as lamb, rabbit and duck to perfection. Expect local, organic and seasonal ingredients, and a killer wine list. Reservations recommended. (📞503-538-8880; www.tinasdundee.com; 760 Hwy 99W; mains $29-46; ⏰5-9pm)

Shopping

Velour   VINTAGE

13 🔒 MAP P134, G5

Americana folk meets Pacific Northwest heritage at Velour, an aesthetic-forward lifestyle shop curating vintage and handmade clothing, jewelry and accessories, plus a selection of small home-wares. Think vintage Danner hiking boots, canvas military backpacks, voile lace dresses, '70s band tees, rattan baskets and a healthy selection of buffalo plaid. Quality and artisanship are standard, no matter what you score. (📞503-718-8118; www.shopvelour.com; 716 E 1st St; ⏰11am-6pm Mon-Sat)

Red Hills Market (p137)

Explore ◈
Salem

The state capital is a peaceful university city that makes a good day trip from Portland, as it's just an hour's drive south. Highlights include the state capitol and a few museums, along with a riverfront park complete with carousel. Outside the city limits are more interesting destinations, including a spectacular state park, a hilltop abbey and a beautiful themed garden.

The Short List

○ **Trail of Ten Falls Loop (p144)** *Hiking this sublime trail in Silver Falls State Park – and walking behind waterfalls.*

○ **Breitenbush Hot Springs (p146)** *Soaking your tired muscles in the healing waters.*

○ **Oregon Garden (p144)** *Exploring 80 acres of varied and gorgeous gardens on foot or by tram.*

○ **Mount Angel (p145)** *Taking in this Bavarian-style town with a tranquil hilltop abbey and a rocking Oktoberfest.*

○ **Oregon State Capitol (p146)** *Getting to the heart of the state of Oregon by touring this art deco building.*

Getting There & Around

🚆 Trains to/from Portland ($16, 1½ hours, nine daily) stop at the Amtrak station.

🚌 Greyhound services also depart from the Amtrak station for Portland ($14, one hour, four daily).

Salem Map on p142

Oregon State Capitol building, and Capitol Fountain
by Weltzin B Blix, sculptor BOB POOL/SHUTTERSTOCK ©

Willamette Mission State Park

Willamette River

Salem

Chemeketa St NE

Court St NE

Ferry St SE 15 ⊗

Elsinore Theatre

◉ 10

Wilson Park

State St

11 ⊙ Oregon State Capitol

Trade St SE

4 ◉

Hallie Ford Museum of Art

Commercial St SE

Liberty St SE

High St SE

Church St SE

Winter St SE

5 Willamette ◉ Heritage Center

Capitol St NE

12th St NE

Willamette University

Leslie St SE

Pringle Park

0 ———————————— 400 m
0 ———————————— 0.2 miles

See Salem Enlargement

Salem ◉

⊗ 14

◉ 9

State St

Cordon Rd NE

State St

Willamette Valley

12th St SE

Mission St E

Lancaster Dr SE

16 🛈

River Rd S

Liberty Rd S

MadronaAve

SE

22

N Santiam Hwy SE

Sunnyside Rd SE

Battle Creek Rd SE

5

Mill Creek Rd SE

8 Enchanted
◉ Forest

13 ◉ Willamette Valley Vineyards

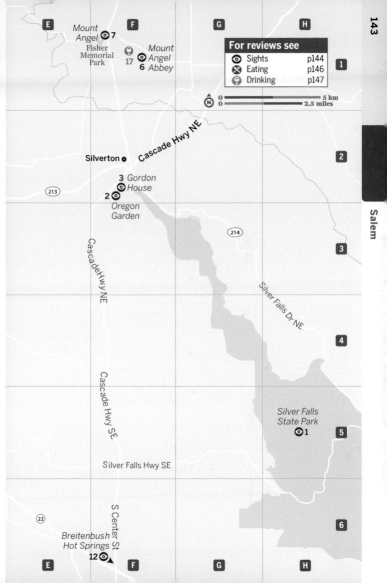

Salem

E
F
G
H

Mount Angel ⊙7
Fisher Memorial Park
17
Mount Angel Abbey
6

For reviews see
⊙ Sights   p144
✕ Eating   p146
🍺 Drinking   p147

1

0   5 km
0   2.5 miles

Cascade Hwy NE

Silverton ⊙

2

3 Gordon House
2 ⊙
Oregon Garden

(213)

(214)

3

Cascade Hwy NE

Silver Falls Dr NE

4

Cascade Hwy SE

Silver Falls Hwy SE

Silver Falls State Park
⊙1

5

(22)

S Center St

Breitenbush Hot Springs
12 ⊙

6

E
F
G
H

Sights

Silver Falls State Park

PARK

1 ◉ MAP P142, H5

Oregon's largest state park, Silver Falls, located 26 miles east of Salem on Hwy 214, is an easy day trip from Portland, Salem and Eugene. It offers camping, swimming, picnicking, cycling and horseback riding. Best of all are the hikes, the most famous being the **Trail of Ten Falls Loop**, a relatively easy 8-mile loop that winds up a basalt canyon through thick forests filled with ferns, moss and wildflowers. (☎503-873-8681; www.oregonstateparks.org; day fee $5, tent sites/RV sites/cabins $19/29/43)

Oregon Garden

GARDENS

2 ◉ MAP P142, F2

Plant lovers shouldn't miss this garden, located 15 miles east of Salem outside Silverton. Over 20 specialty gardens are showcased on 80 acres, including a Northwest plant collection, miniature conifer section, children's garden and even a pet-friendly garden. There are 5 miles of walking trails, with a tram that runs on weekends for those with mobility issues. Be sure to check the website for events like classes and lectures. Opening hours and admission prices vary year-round. (☎503-874-8100; www.oregongarden.org; 879 W Main St; adult/student $14/8; ☉9am-6pm)

Gordon House

HISTORIC SITE

3 ◉ MAP P142, F2

Next to the Oregon Garden in Silverton is the Gordon House, the only building in Oregon designed by Frank Lloyd Wright. It was built in 1964 and moved to its present location in 2002. Opening hours and days vary; reservations essential, book ahead online. (☎503-874-6006; www.thegordonhouse.org; 869 W Main St; tours $20; ☉tours noon, 1pm & 2pm)

Hallie Ford Museum of Art

MUSEUM

4 ◉ MAP P142, C2

Willamette University's Hallie Ford Museum of Art boasts the state's best collection of Pacific Northwest art, including an impressive Native American gallery. (☎503-370-6855; www.willamette.edu/arts/hfma; 700 State St; adult/child $6/free, Tue free; ☉10am-5pm Tue-Sat, 1-5pm Sun)

Willamette Heritage Center

MUSEUM

5 ◉ MAP P142, C2

This interesting 5-acre complex houses grassy gardens, two gift shops, a clutch of pioneer buildings and two museums. The Mission Mill Museum, Jason Lee House (1841), John Boon House (1847), Methodist Parsonage (1841) and an old Presbyterian church (1858) all look pretty much as they did in the 1840s and 1850s. The Thomas Kay Woolen Mill was built in 1889 and was powered by a mill race (water-way), a section of which still runs through the grounds. (☏503-585-7012; www.willametteheritage.org; 1313 Mill St SE; adult/child $8/4; ⏰10am-5pm Mon-Sat)

Mount Angel Abbey MONASTERY

6 ◉ MAP P142, F1

Open to everyone, the Mount Angel Abbey is a delightful Benedictine monastery on grassy grounds set atop a hill that overlooks town. There's a modernist library designed by Finnish architect Alvar Aalto, plus a quirky museum featuring a 2.5lb pig hairball and deformed calves (among other amazing taxidermy). Lodging is available to those seeking a spiritual retreat, and the monks brew their own Belgian-style beers at Benedictine Brewery (p147), adjacent to the abbey grounds. (☏503-845-3030; www.mountangelabbey.org; 1 Abbey Dr; ⏰9am-5pm)

Mount Angel AREA

7 ◉ MAP P142, F1

Eighteen miles north of Salem, the little town of Mount Angel, with its Bavarian-style storefronts and lovely abbey, is like an old-world holdover in the Oregon countryside. Visit in mid- to late September, during **Oktoberfest** (www.oktoberfest.org; day passes $5-15), for maximum effect; thousands show up for the music, beer and dances. Gothic-like **St Mary Parish Church** (1910) is worth a visit for its mural-covered walls. (www.mtangel.org)

Enchanted Forest AMUSEMENT PARK

8 ◉ MAP P142, B6

Located 7 miles south of Salem, this children's theme park is a fun fantasyland offering rides (extra charge), a European village, a Western town and storybook themes, among other things. There are water light shows and a comedy theater in summer. Picnic grounds, gift shops and food services are also here. Opening hours vary widely so check the website for details. (☏503-371-4242; www.enchantedforest.com; 8462 Enchanted Way SE; adult/child $13.50/12, ride tickets $1; ⏰10am-4pm, longer hours in summer)

Bush's Pasture Park PARK

9 ◉ MAP P142, B4

One of Oregon's leading citizens of the late 19th century was Asahel Bush, a newspaperman and highly successful banker who began building his rambling Italianate residence in 1877. Designed to be a self-sufficient farm, the grounds are now preserved as Bush's Pasture Park and include a large rose garden, a playground, picnic areas and walking trails. (890 Mission St SE)

Elsinore Theatre HISTORIC BUILDING

10 ◉ MAP P142, B2

This dazzling Tudor-Gothic landmark, opened in 1926 and once a silent-movie theater, is now primarily a venue for theater and concerts. Classic movies are shown weekly from October to May, with live accompaniment (for silent movies) on a 1778-pipe Wurlitzer organ – one of the finest in the country. Tours by appointment. (📞503-375-3574; www.elsinoretheatre.com; 170 High St SE)

Oregon State Capitol

NOTABLE BUILDING

11 ⊚ MAP P142, C2

The state's first capitol building burned down in 1855, and a domed classic Roman edifice was built to replace it. Unfortunately, that building also burned down (in 1935), and the current capitol building was completed in 1938. Bauhaus and art deco influences are apparent, especially in the strident bas-relief in the front statuary and the hatbox-like cupola. The building is faced with white Danby Vermont marble, and the interior is lined with rose travertine from Montana. (📞503-986-1388; www.oregonlegislature.gov; 900 Court St NE; admission free; 🕑8am-5pm Mon-Fri)

Breitenbush Hot Springs

HOT SPRINGS

12 ⊚ MAP P142, F6

Enjoy salubrious climes at Breitenbush Hot Springs, a fancy spa with massages, yoga and the like. Day-use activities include the hot springs and sauna, yoga and meditation, massage, hiking trails and a library. You can also stay the night here. Reservations are required, including for day use. (📞503-854-3320; www.breitenbush.com; 53000 Breitenbush Rd; day use per person

$23-39, children under 3 free; 🕑office 9am-4pm Mon-Sat)

Willamette Valley Vineyards

WINE

13 ⊚ MAP P142, B6

One of Oregon's most-respected wine growers is Willamette Valley Vineyards, on an imposing hilltop south of town. (📞503-588-9463; www.wvv.com; 8800 Enchanted Way; flights $10-15; 🕑11am-6pm Sun-Thu, to 8pm Fri & Sat)

Eating

Word of Mouth Bistro

BISTRO $

14 🍴 MAP P142, B4

If crème brûlée French toast sounds good, then make a beeline for this friendly and excellent bistro. Other tasty treats include cinnamon roll pancakes, an asparagus and Brie omelet, toasted breakfast burritos and a filet mignon Benedict. Gourmet sandwiches, salads and burgers use the lunch menu (weekdays only). (📞503-930-4285; www.wordofsalem.com; 140 17th St NE; mains $9-16; 🕑7am-3pm Wed-Sun)

Wild Pear

DELI $

15 🍴 MAP P142, B1

A popular deli, Wild Pear serves up tasty soups, sandwiches and salads, along with fancier options like a lobster melt. There's also a Greek wrap, a charcuterie plate, pizzas, homemade pastries and even a traditional pho (Vietnamese noodle soup) – all combined with good, efficient service. (📞503-378-7515; www.wildpearcatering.com; 372 State St; mains $11-15; 🕐10:30am-6:30pm Mon-Sat)

Drinking

Santiam Brewing   BREWERY

16 🍺 MAP P142, B4

Fans of British brews and bites should head to this lively taproom tucked in a nondescript industrial complex. Santiam has a dedicated cask-ale bar and slings craft beers and ciders along with a full menu of British and American pub fare. Expect scotch eggs, Welsh rarebit, shepherd's pie and spotted dick, plus burgers, a Philly cheesesteak and poutine. (📞503-689-1260; www.santiambrewing.com; 2544 19th St SE;

pub food mains $13-16; 🕐11am-10pm Sun-Wed, to 11pm Thu-Sat)

Benedictine Brewery   BREWERY

17 🍺 MAP P142, F1

At Benedictine, 18 miles northeast of Salem, the monks of Mount Angel Abbey (p145) brew Belgian-style beers using centuries-old monastic traditions. One of three monk-operated breweries in the country, they use water drawn from the abbey well and hops that have grown on the grounds since the 1880s. The brewery's serene Saint Michael's Taproom was constructed by volunteers using Douglas Fir timber from the abbey's tree farm. (📞971-343-2772; www.benedictinebrewery.com; 400 Humpert Lane; 🕐2-7pm Wed & Thu, 1-8pm Fri & Sat, 11am-5pm Sun)

Silver Falls State Park (p144)

DAN SHERWOOD/GETTY IMAGES ©

Survival Guide

Before You Go

Book Your Stay

○ Plan on paying extra (at least $25 per day) for parking at downtown and Lloyd Center hotels.

○ Rates at top-end hotels vary depending on day of the week.

○ Reservations are a good idea in summer.

○ There's a handful of hostels and atmospheric guesthouses in more residential areas.

Useful Websites

Travel Portland (www.travelportland.com) Lists lodging options by district.

Shift Vacation Rentals (www.shiftvacation rentals.com) Local-run vacation rental homes.

Lonely Planet (www.lonelyplanet.com/usa/pacific-northwest/portland) Reviews and recommendations.

Best Budget

The Society Hotel (www.thesociety hotel.com) Bunks with

Portland

When to Go

○ Portland's **summer** (June to September) sees festivals galore, including the Oregon Brewers Festival and the Bite of Oregon.

○ Enjoy museums, galleries and coffee shops during the **rainy season** (October to March).

○ Long-awaited **spring** flowers reach peak bloom between April and May.

boutique style in Old Town Chinatown.

Hawthorne Portland Hostel (www.portland hostel.org) Ecofriendly, with a great Hawthorne location.

White Eagle (www.mc menamins.com/white-eagle-saloon-hotel) Supposedly haunted saloon with charm.

Friendly Bike Guesthouse (www.friendly bikeguesthouse.com) Bike-friendly digs in a historic house.

Best Midrange

Ace Hotel (www.ace hotel.com/portland) Super stylish with an underground bar.

Benson Hotel (www.bensonhotel.com) Elegant downtown hotel with top-notch service.

Crystal Hotel (www.mcmenamins.com/crystal-hotel) Themed rooms dedicated to the creatives who performed at the neighboring Crystal Ballroom.

Kennedy School (www.mcmenamins.com/kennedy-school) Sleep in a classroom in this former elementary school.

Best Top End

Woodlark (www.wood larkhotel.com) Two historic buildings became one for this ultra-chic downtown boutique.

Heathman Hotel
(www.heathmanhotel.
com) Centrally located,
with luxurious design
and an impressive
library.

Lion & the Rose (www.
lionrose.com) Stately
B&B in a quiet, historic
neighborhood.

Hoxton (www.the
hoxton.com) Super-hip
design and good bars,
priced on the lower
end of the boutique
spectrum.

Arriving in Portland

Portland International Airport
Portland International Airport (503-460-4234; www.flypdx.com; 7000 NE Airport Way; ; Red) is located about 10 miles northeast of downtown. There are direct flights and connections to most major airports in the country, plus some direct international flights.

Union Station
Amtrak departs from **Union Station** (800-872-7245; www.

amtrak.com; 800 NW 6th Ave; 17, Green, Yellow), and offers services up and down the West Coast, plus a cross-continental line.

Greyhound Depot
Greyhound buses leave from this **depot** (Map p88; 503-243-2361; www.greyhound.com; 550 NW 6th Ave; Green, Orange, Yellow) and connect Portland with cities along I-5 and I-84.

If you're traveling between Portland, Seattle and Vancouver, BC, try **Bolt Bus** (Map p72; 877-265-8287; www.boltbus.com), which provides service in large buses with wi-fi.

Getting Around

Bicycle
Portland is often named the most bike-friendly city in the US.

Check out **Everybody's Bike Rentals & Tours** (Map p88; 503-358-0152; www.pdxbikerentals.com; 305 NE Wygant St; rentals per hour $8-25; 10am-5pm; 6). For city bike maps, see

www.portlandoregon.gov/transportation.

Portland's bike-share program is **Biketown** (www.biketownpdx.com). After a set-up fee of $5, the rate is 8¢ a minute, with a $2 charge for locking it at any public rack inside the system area ($10 if locked anywhere outside the system). If you return the bike to a kiosk, you earn a $1 credit. There's an app available for locating bikes and making easy payments.

Bus
The **TriMet** (www.trimet.org) bus system has 84 lines through Portland. Interactive schedules and maps are available on the website, and TriMet's tracker app lets you see details for every bus stop in the city in real time.

Car & Motorcycle
Parking on the east side of the city is generally easy; downtown, SmartPark garages, some with electric-vehicle charging stations, offer affordable parking (see www.

portlandoregon.gov/transportation/35272). Downtown, Northwest and the Pearl District often have metered parking; finding a spot here can be harder.

It only became legal to pump your own gasoline in Oregon in 2019. Most stations have free full-serve attendants on-site.

Major car-rental agencies have outlets downtown and at the airport. **Zipcar** (www.zipcar.com; membership fee per month from $7, rental per hour from $8.50) is a popular car-sharing option.

Taxi

Cabs are available 24 hours by phone. **Broadway Cab** (☏503-333-3333; www.broadwaycab.com) and **Radio Cab** (☏503-227-1212; www.radiocab.net) are two reliable operators. Rideshare services are abundant.

Train

The MAX light rail connects to most of the major metro areas (and suburbs) and are easily navigable. Buses connect with many stops.

The Portland Street Car runs downtown

and near the river on the eastern side. For maps and trip planning for all of these, download the app for TriMet.

Essential Information

Accessible Travel

Portland in general is widely accessible for travelers with disabilities; for information on getting around town by light rail or bus, call ☏503-962-2455 or email accessible@trimet.org.

To increase access to cycling, Biketown has a program called **Adaptive Biketown** (www.adaptivebiketown.com) that rents hand- and foot-powered recumbent bikes through a local agency.

Inside the **Travel Portland** (Map p38; ☏503-275-8355; www.travelportland.com; 701 SW 6th Ave; ⊙8:30am-5:30pm Mon-Fri, 10am-4pm Sat Nov-Apr, plus 10am-2pm Sun May-Oct; ☐Red, Blue, Green, Yellow) visitor center at Pioneer Courthouse Square,

there's a high-tech, all-gender, ADA-accessible restroom with an attendant on duty.

Download Lonely Planet's free Accessible Travel guides from https://shop.lonelyplanet.com/categories/accessible-travel.com.

Business Hours

The following hours are a general guide – check individual listings for specifics.

Restaurants Breakfast 7am to 11:30am, lunch 11:30am to 2pm, dinner 5 to 9pm

Shops 9am to 5pm (malls to 9pm) Monday to Friday; sometimes more limited hours on weekends

Banks 9am or 10am to 5pm or 6pm weekdays; some also 10am to 2pm Saturday

Supermarkets 7am to 10pm; sometimes 24-hr

Discount Cards

Family Fun Pass (www.familyfunpass.org) Enables discounted access to attractions around Portland and the Willamette Valley. Passes start at $49 for a group of four.

Electricity

Type A
120V/60Hz

Type B
120V/60Hz

Important Holidays

New Year's Day
January 1

Martin Luther King Jr Day Third Monday in January

Presidents' Day Third Monday in February

Easter March/April

Memorial Day Last Monday in May

LGBTIQ+ Pride Third weekend following Memorial Day

Independence Day (Fourth of July) July 4

Labor Day First Monday in September

Indigenous People's Day Second Monday in October

Halloween October 31

Veterans' Day November 11

Thanksgiving Day Fourth Thursday in November

Christmas Day December 25

New Year's Eve December 31

Money

ATMs are abundant. Many bars, restaurants and grocery stores also have them, but fees are steep ($3 to $5, plus your own bank's fees).

Tipping

Tipping in the US is *not* optional, as most service-industry workers make only the minimum wage and rely almost entirely on tips for their income. However, if service is truly terrible, tip less than 15% or reduce the following standard amounts.

Responsible Travel

Portland has always been a pioneer in the area of urban sustainability. There is a ban on single-use plastics; carry a reusable bag whenever you're out shopping.

Try to support businesses using sustainable practices. Portland's food scene in particular is well-known for putting locally grown, sustainably raised ingredients at the heart of everything. Supporting small, local businesses is another way to support local communities.

Examples of sustainable local attractions include **Pickathon** (www.pickathon.com; 16581 SE HagenRd, Happy Valley; weekendpass $325; ⊙Aug), a family-friendly, single-use-plastic-free music festival; **Courier Coffee**

Roasters (☎503-545-6444; www.couriercoffeeroasters.com; 923 SW Oak St; ☺7am-6pm Mon-Fri, 9am-5pm Sat& Sun; ☎), which delivers roasted beans by bicycle; and **Bamboo Sushi** (☎503-232-5255; www.bamboosushi.com; 310 SE 28th Ave; mains $11-26, nigiri $5-10; ☺4:30-10pm; ☎20), which claims to be the world's first 'certified sustainable' sushi restaurant.

Safe Travel

COVID-19 travel protocols are subject to change. For updated information on requirements for travel to/within the US, visit the CDC website (www.cdc.gov/coronavirus) and www.canitravel.net.

Current COVID-19 protocols for Portland can be found at https://govstatus.egov.com/or-oha-face-coverings. Masks are mandatory only in public health facilities, but strongly recommended on public transportation. Some local businesses and venues may require proof of vaccination as a condition of entry.

Bartenders $1 to $2 per drink, or 15% of the bill. Note: good tippers get stronger drinks.

Bellhops $2 per bag, plus $5 to $10 extra for special service.

Housekeeping staff $2 to $5 daily, left on the pillow each day; more if you're messy.

Parking valets $2; extra for special service.

Restaurant servers 15% to 20% of the pretax bill.

Taxis and rideshares 10% to 15% of the metered fare.

Toilets

Toilets are easy to find in Portland – shops and restaurants usually require a purchase.

There is an 11-stall restroom inside the Travel Portland visitor center.

Tourist Information

Travel Portland (Map p38; ☎503-275-8355; www.travelportland.com; 701 SW 6th Ave, Pioneer Courthouse Sq; ☺8:30am-5:30pm Mon-Fri, 10am-4pm Sat Nov-Apr, plus 10am-2pm

Sun May-Oct; ☒Red, Blue, Green, Yellow) Has superfriendly volunteers staffing this office. There's a small theater with a 12-minute film about the city, and there are **TriMet** (Map p38; ☎503-725-9005, 503-238-7433; www.trimet.org; ☺8:30am-5:30pm Mon-Fri) bus and light-rail offices inside.

Visas

For up-to-date information about visas and immigration, check the US Department of State (www.travel.state.gov) and the travel section of US Customs & Border Protection (www.cbp.gov).

Most foreign visitors need a visa to enter the US. You can determine your eligibility for a Waiver of Tourist Visa (VWT) with the Electronic System for Travel Authorization (ESTA; www.cbp.gov/travel/international-visitors/esta). Visitors should carry their passport (valid for at least six months) and expect to be photographed and have their index fingers scanned.

Behind the Scenes

Send Us Your Feedback

We love to hear from travelers – your comments help make our books better. We read every word, and we guarantee that your feedback goes straight to the authors. Visit **lonelyplanet.com/contact** to submit your updates and suggestions.

Note: We may edit, reproduce and incorporate your comments in Lonely Planet products such as guidebooks, websites and digital products, so let us know if you are happy to have your name acknowledged. For a copy of our privacy policy visit lonelyplanet.com/legal.

Celeste's Thanks

Thanks to my husband Josh and my kids who have come with me on so many Oregon trips over the years. And to many friends old and new that helped out this time around, including Ticari, Chris and Ashley, Nathan, Dana, Jon and Kara, Ron and Nisa, Elizabeth, Pattye, Rachel Cabakoff, Amanda Castleman, Dave Nevins, Amy Hunter, all my LP co-authors and Ben Buckner for seeing this through.

Acknowledgements

Cover photograph: Sun rising over a vineyard, Willamette Valley, Steven Madow/Shutterstock ©

Back cover photograph: Portland Oregon sign, Portland, Png Studio Photography/Shutterstock ©

This Book

This 2nd edition of Lonely Planet's *Pocket Portland & the Willamette Valley* guidebook was curated by Celeste Brash and researched and written by Celeste and MaSovaida Morgan, with additional contributions by Anthony Ham. This guidebook was produced by the following:

Destination Editor
Ben Buckner

Commissioning Editor
Sasha Drew

Senior Product Editors
Grace Dobell, Kathryn Rowan

Regional Senior Cartographer Alison Lyall

Product Editors Andrea Dobbin, Hannah Cartmel

Book Designers Norma Brewer, Virginia Moreno

Assisting Editors Sarah Bailey, James Bainbridge, Alex Conroy, Carly Hall, Gabrielle Innes, Lou McGregor, Monique Perrin, Sarah Reid, Gabrielle Stefanos

Cartographers Diana Von Holdt, Julie Sheridan

Cover Researcher
Lauren Egan

Thanks to Victoria Harrison, Andi Jones, Sonia Kapoor, Kate Mathews, Jenna Myers, Lauren O'Connell, Vicky Smith

Index

See also separate subindexes for:

⊗ **Eating p158**

○ **Drinking p159**

☆ **Entertainment p159**

⊕ **Shopping p159**

Our Writers

Celeste Brash

Like many California natives, Celeste now lives in Portland. She arrived, however, after 15 years in French Polynesia, a year and a half in Southeast Asia and a stint teaching English as a second language (in an American accent) in Brighton, England – among other things. She's been writing guidebooks for Lonely Planet since 2005 and her travel articles have appeared in publications from BBC Travel to *National Geographic*. She's currently writing a book about her five years on a remote pearl farm in the Tuamotu Atolls and is represented by the Donald Maass Agency, New York.

MaSovaida Morgan

MaSovaida is a travel writer and multimedia storyteller whose wanderlust has taken her to more than 40 countries and all seven continents. Previously, she was Lonely Planet's Destination Editor for South America and Antarctica for four years and worked as an editor for newspapers and NGOs in the Middle East and United Kingdom. Follow her on Instagram @MaSovaida.

Contributing Writer Anthony Ham wrote the Under the Radar Portland feature and updated the Survial Guide.

Published by Lonely Planet Global Limited
CRN 554153
2nd edition – Nov 2022
ISBN 978 1 78868 458 3
© Lonely Planet 2022 Photographs © as indicated 2022
10 9 8 7 6 5 4 3 2 1
Printed in Singapore

Survival Guide

NYC bikeshare (p244) PISAPHOTOGRAPHY/SHUTTERSTOCK ©

Before You Go

Book Your Stay

o Year-round, expect high prices for tiny spaces. Many hotels add a 'facility' or 'resort' fee to the base rate.

o Highest rates are typically September through New Year's, plus long holiday weekends; generally lowest: February and July. Conventions or special events can also cause price spikes.

o Brooklyn and Queens (especially near Queens Plaza) offer better value. Hostels are scarce.

o See www.lonelyplanet. com/usa/new-york-city/ hotels for more recommendations.

Best Budget

Local (www.thelocalny. com) Affordable dorms and doubles with rooftop views and a fringe-cool Long Island City location.

Harlem Flophouse (www.harlemflophouse. com) Old-school style works its charms inside

New York City

°C/°F Temp   Rainfall inches/mm

When to Go

Spring (Mar–May) Hit-or-miss weather; when it hits, and parks bloom, the mood is infectious.

Fall (Sep–Nov) Warm days, cooler nights, autumn leaves, and the best formal arts programming.

Summer (Jun–Aug) Hot, humid and, yes, a little smelly. Brimming with free concerts, movies and more.

Winter (Dec–Mar) Gray, cold and windy, sometimes snowy, but holiday season is festive.

this beautiful Harlem brownstone.

Carlton Arms (www. carltonarms.com) Come for the low prices; stay for the 54 eclectically painted rooms (or vice versa).

NY Moore Hostel (www.nymoore hostel.com) Clean and friendly, on the doorstep of fab nightlife in Brooklyn's East Williamsburg.

Best Midrange

Freehand New York (www.freehandhotels. com/new-york) Well-priced rooms with a

handcrafted style, near the Flatiron District.

Boro Hotel (www. borohotel.com) On a residential block, incongruous high design with great views in Long Island City.

Arthouse Hotel NYC (www.arthousehotel nyc.com) Tiny rooms don't matter with Lincoln Center as a lounge and Central Park as a backyard.

Citizen M (www. citizenm.com) Modern, high-tech rooms near Times Square's heart.

TWA Hotel (www. twahotel.com) Stay at

JFK for jet-set style in the iconic 1960s Eero Saarinen TWA terminal.

Ace Hotel Brooklyn (www.acehotel.com/brooklyn) Hang with locals in the buzzy lobby and restaurant; catch z's in the stylish rooms.

Best Top End

Greenwich Hotel (www.thegreenwich hotel.com) Elegant and eclectic, yet under-stated: the only thing splashy at Robert de Niro's hotel is the lantern-lit pool.

Giraffe (www.hotel giraffe.com) Not any kind of scene, but com-fortable and homey, with free snacks.

Knickerbocker (www. theknickerbocker. com) Minimalist luxe is a respite after a busy city day, so is the fab rooftop bar.

W New York Union Square (www.wnew yorkunionsquare.com) A 1911 beauty turned semi-hip, with a perfect location.

Bowery Hotel (www. theboweryhotel.com) 19th-century ambience finds modern expres-sion in the East Village.

Wythe Hotel (www. wythehotel.com) Former-factory-turned-upscale-hotel with an acclaimed brasserie that's more Left Bank than East River.

Arriving in New York City

John F Kennedy International Airport (JFK)

○ AirTrain connects to subway or Long Island Railroad (LIRR). Travel time to Manhattan is about an hour.

○ AirTrain does not use OMNY (yet); fare is $8, plus $1 for the Metro-card; buy at machines as you exit. Subway fare additional $2.75 (use OMNY or add on Metro-card). LIRR fares from $5 (off-peak; buy from trackside machines).

○ For Midtown and Downtown Brooklyn: AirTrain to Jamaica, then LIRR direct to Penn Station and Atlantic Terminal, respectively.

○ For Harlem, Upper East Side, Lower East Side: AirTrain to Jamaica, then subway ($2.75).

○ For most of Brooklyn, Lower Manhattan, West Village and Upper West Side: AirTrain to Howard Beach, then subway.

○ Taxis to Manhattan cost a flat $52 ($56.50 4pm to 8pm), plus tolls, tip.

○ Shuttle vans run to Grand Central or Port Authority (about $45 per person).

○ If you have more than one suitcase, avoid the subway; many stations lack elevators.

LaGuardia Airport (LGA)

○ M60 bus ($2.75) runs across 125th St in Man-hattan; free transfer to subway. Best for Harlem or Upper East or West Sides.

○ Q70 bus (free) runs to Jackson Heights, for subway ($2.75) or LIRR. Best for all other Man-hattan destinations.

○ Taxis range from $35 to $55, excluding tolls and tip.

○ Shuttle vans to Mid-town cost around $27 per person.

OMNY vs Metrocard

All subway stations and buses have the convenient OMNY system: tap-and-go with your own credit or debit card or phone. (Stored-value OMNY cards are also available from Walgreen's and CVS.) You get one free transfer (between subway and bus or bus to bus) within two hours. Starting each Monday, after 12 rides (totaling $33), anything else the rest of the week is free.

If you're arriving midweek, consider the legacy Metrocard (until it phases out in 2024). Its weekly pass ($33, plus $1 for the card) starts whenever you first swipe.

Newark Liberty International Airport (EWR)

o Similar distance from Midtown as JFK, but transit is more expensive.

o AirTrain to the Newark Airport station, then buy NJ Transit ticket to New York Penn Station (don't confuse with *Newark* Penn Station) for $15.50.

o Shuttle van service to Midtown for around $42 per person.

o Taxis to Manhattan range from $50 to $70, but add in tolls (at least $15), tip and other fees (large bags, rush hours, East-Side Manhattan addresses). For destinations south of 34th St,

shared taxis ($18 to $26 per person) are an option.

Getting Around

Addresses

In Manhattan street addresses, note the W or E: this denotes west or east of Fifth Ave (with building numbers increasing the further you go from Fifth).

On Foot

o If you're able, walking is efficient, and Manhattan's grid system makes navigation simple.

o Estimate walking time at one minute for each street and three minutes for each avenue.

Subway

o Inexpensive, efficient and running 24 hours, though sometimes tricky to navigate.

o A single fare ($2.75, anywhere in the system) includes a free transfer (between subway and bus, or bus-to-bus) within two hours.

o Kids under 44" (short enough to walk under the turnstile) ride free.

Bus

o Handy for crossing Manhattan east–west. Also nice for sightseeing.

o Rides cost $2.75. Board at front, tap on OMNY reader (or dip Metrocard) and get off at back.

o Select Bus Service (SBS) routes run on major thoroughfares such as 14th St and 125th St. Board at any door and tap on OMNY readers onboard. With Metrocard (or coins), buy a ticket from sidewalk machines before boarding.

Devilish Subway Details

Lines New Yorkers refer to train lines by their number or letter, not by color. A shared color indicates trains that run a similar route but branch outside Manhattan and/or offer local or express service.

Express vs local Express trains stop only at major stations (white circles on the map); local trains stop at smaller ones (black dots) as well.

Which track? On a given platform with express and local trains, express trains run on the inner tracks (away from the wall) and local trains arrive on the outer ones; double-check signs above each track.

Entrances At street level, signs may say 'Downtown only' or 'Uptown only': you cannot cross to the other platform below ground. If you enter on the wrong side you will have to go back up and reenter on the correct side -- and pay again (or beg a booth attendant for mercy).

Lamps At station entrances, a green lamp means the entrance is open 24 hours. A red lamp means it's closed at night.

Nights and weekends Some express lines turn local, and some lines don't run at all. Unfortunately these changes are not shown on posted maps, and only cryptically described on signs above tracks. Check www.mta.info for weekend maps and other service disruptions.

Taxi & Rideshare

Yellow taxis Plentiful in Manhattan; scarcer elsewhere. Expect at least $12 to $15 across Manhattan and $20 to $25 for the nearest Brooklyn or Queens destination (plus bridge or tunnel tolls). There's $1 peak surcharge (weekdays 4pm to 8pm), but no fee for bags.

Green taxis Same rates, but can pick up only in the outer boroughs and above 96th St in Manhattan. Drivers can be reluctant to

go into Manhattan, but are legally obliged to.

Passenger rights You have the right to, among other things, your preferred route, no music, and air-con or heat. The driver must accept service animals and may not refuse service based on destination. If you have a problem, note the driver's license number for a complaint to the TLC (call 311).

Uber / Lyft Fares are on par with or higher than taxis, but the apps

can be handy in neighborhoods where taxis are scarcer. Uber has partnered with the city, so you may end up with a yellow cab anyway.

Curb app Summons a yellow or green taxi (immediately or scheduled); rates are approximately 30% higher than meter fare.

Car service 'Black cars' charge flat fares and cannot be hailed on the street; they must be called. They're good for scheduled rides – to the airport, for

Taxi Tips

Roof light Look for the number mounted on the top of the cab. If it's lit, the taxi is available; if dark, it's off-duty or full.

Destination Tell the driver after you're in the car.

Seating Maximum passengers is four. Fill the backseat first.

Shift change Avoid 3pm to 5pm, if possible; there is always a car shortage, and fares incur $1 surcharge.

Payment At end of ride, with cash or credit card (via the touch screen in back).

Tipping 10% or 15%, more if driver handles luggage.

instance. In Brooklyn, try **Northside** (www.northsidecarservice.com) in Williamsburg and **Arecibo** (www.aricbocc.com) in Park Slope.

Bicycle

o NYC has hundreds of miles of bike lanes, but car traffic (and ebike and moped traffic) is fierce. Less-experienced city riders should stick to riverside greenways.

o Most bike shops have free city-printed bike maps, or see NYC Bike Maps (www.nycbike-maps.com).

o Helmets required for children 13 and under.

o Bike-share network Citi Bike (www.citibikenyc.com) covers Manhattan and parts of Brooklyn and Queens. Single rides are pricey ($4 for 30 minutes); 24-hour pass is $15. Ebikes cost more. Use Google Maps for routing; the Citi Bike app's routing feature (oddly/dangerously!) does not prioritize bike lanes.

Boat

NYC Ferry (www.ferry.nyc) Via Pier 11 near Wall St, boats link all five boroughs, with views and fresh air. Service can be infrequent; download the app to

plan ahead with schedules. Single fares (buy in app or at docks) are $4, good for two hours in one direction; 10 tickets are $27.50; bikes ride free. Note: there is no free transfer to/from subways and buses.

Staten Island Ferry (www.siferry.com) Free, frequent, commuter-oriented ferry between Lower Manhattan and Staten Island. Runs 24/7. Worth an out-and-back ride for the view of the Statue of Liberty.

Essential Information

Accessible Travel

o All major museums and cultural centers are accessible.

o Some, but not all, Broadway venues have provisions for theater-goers with disabilities.

o In winter, sidewalks are inconsistently cleared of snow and curb cuts can be blocked by slush.

o Very few subway stations (mostly major transfer stations) have elevators, and they

can be dirty and poorly placed. Buses are a better bet (all 'kneel' and have space for chairs in front). See www.mta.info/accessibility for more.

○ Order accessible taxis through **Accessible Dispatch** (http://accessibledispatch.com), which also has an app.

○ Download Lonely Planet's free Accessible Travel guides from https://shop.lonelyplanet.com/categories/accessible-travel.com.

Business Hours

Standard business hours are as follows:

Banks
9am–6pm Monday–Friday, some also 9am–noon Saturday

Bars
5pm–2am, some to 4am

Businesses
9am–5pm Monday–Friday

Clubs
10pm–4am

Restaurants
Breakfast 6am–11am, lunch noon to around 3pm, and dinner 5–11pm. Weekend brunch 10am–4pm.

Shops
10am to around 7pm weekdays, 11am to around 8pm Saturday; Sundays variable. (Some close - others keep weekday hours). Downtown stores usually stay open later.

Discount Cards

Two options, one simple and one more complex, offering flat-fee admission to major attractions. Make your own priority list and then run the numbers.

New York CityPASS (www.citypass.com) From a short list of museums and observation decks, select five over nine days (adult/child $132/112), or three in three days (adult/child $94/74).

New York Pass (www.newyorkpass.com) and **GoCity** (www.gocity.com) are the same company, with a much longer list of options, but pricier (1–10 days $139 to $473). Better for visitors with a long bucket list and lots of energy.

Electricity

Type A
120V/60Hz

Type B
120V/60Hz

Legal Matters

o You are not obligated to speak to a police officer if you don't wish to, but never walk away from an officer until given permission (politely ask if you are free to leave).

o If arrested, you have the right to one phone call. If you don't have a lawyer or family member to help, call your consulate.

o You are permitted to take photos or videos of police.

Etiquette

Greetings Acknowledge nearby staff when entering or leaving a business. Further chit-chat not required.

Small talk New Yorkers value time as much as money: if asking a stranger for help, skip pleasantries and go straight to the question.

Hot topics Money and power are enthusiastically discussed. People will ask about your job, how much your hotel costs and what you think of politics.

Traffic flow Sidewalks are for walking, not gawking. If you need to check your phone, step well to the side and let people go by.

Restaurants Servers bring the bill almost directly after dessert; rarely will you have to ask.

More info See Nathan Pyle's charming illustrated *NYC Basic Tips & Etiquette* (2014).

Internet Access

o Free wi-fi at larger public parks: High Line, Bryant Park, Battery Park, City Hall Park, Madison Square Park and Tompkins Square Park. Check www.nycgovparks.org/facilities/wifi for more.

o LinkNYC (www.link.nyc) kiosks offer charging ports and free wi-fi.

o Underground subway stations have wi-fi (aboveground ones do not).

o Most cafes, museums and libraries offer wi-fi.

Important Numbers

Fire, police & ambulance 911

Municipal info (including taxi complaints) 311

Local directory 411

Money

Plastic rules (and Venmo is expanding), but keep cash on you for some small businesses and food carts.

ATMs

o ATMs are in banks and in delis, restaurants, bars and grocery stores (the latter usually charge similar fees to out-of-network banks, $3 to $5).

o Some European banks require cards to be activated for ATM use outside the EU; check before you go.

Changing Money

Banks and money changers such as Travelex, found all over New York City, sell US currency at current exchange rate. Those at airports and tourist sites like Times Square charge higher fees.

Credit Cards

o Accepted at most hotels, restaurants and shops. Some transactions, such as purchasing tickets to performances and renting a car, can't be done without one.

o Handheld terminals at restaurants are increasingly common, but many places will take your card, run it and return it.

Taxes & Refunds

o Posted prices almost never include sales tax (8.875%); it's up to you to factor it in.

o Hotel rooms are subject to 14.75% tax, plus a $2 occupancy fee per night.

o Clothing and footwear under $110 is not taxed.

o The US has no nationwide value-added tax (VAT), so foreign visitors cannot make 'tax-free' purchases.

Tipping

Tipping is *not* optional; only withhold tips in cases of outrageously bad service.

Restaurant servers 18–20%

Bartenders Minimum per drink $1, $2 per specialty cocktail or 15–20% overall

Taxi drivers 10–15%, rounded up to the dollar

Airport & hotel porters $2 per bag, minimum per cart $5

Hotel cleaners $3 to $5 per night, envelope or card may be provided

Public Holidays

New Year's Day January 1

Martin Luther King Day Third Monday in January

Presidents' Day Third Monday in February

Memorial Day Late May

Juneteenth June 19

Independence Day July 4

Labor Day First Monday in September

Veterans Day November 11

Thanksgiving Fourth Thursday in November

Christmas Day December 25

Responsible Travel
Covid-19

o Covid-19 protocols are subject to change. Always check the latest requirements for travel to/within the USA at the CDC website (www.cdc. gov/coronavirus).

o NYC Covid protocols can be found at www. nyc.gov/coronavirus. At the time of writing, some individual theaters and other performance venues were maintaining stricter-than-official policies, so bring proof of vaccination.

Safe Travel

NYC is one of the USA's safest cities, but common sense helps:
o Don't walk alone at night in sparsely populated areas.

o Beware pickpockets in crowds: subways, Times Square, Penn Station.

o The subway is generally safe at all hours, but if it's very late and you're alone, you may want to take a taxi.

o Avoid pressure sales for show tickets and cruises; book online or at official vendors.

Dos & Don'ts

o Don't bother waiting for the 'walk' sign, but do look both ways, especially for bikes. And keep an eye out for cars racing through yellow (and red) lights.

o When opening a taxi door, do check for bikes.

o Do step aside to let passengers off the subway before you board; if you're riding near a door, but it's not your stop, do step off briefly to clear the way.

o Do help people carry big bags or carts up subway stairs: make eye contact, lift the bottom end and go. No need for conversation.

o Don't lean on subway poles; let others use them too.

o Do say it the NY way: wait 'on line,' not 'in line'; meet on *How*-sten Street (Houston St), not *Hugh*-sten. And if a car inches into the crosswalk, you can definitely shout, 'Hey, I'm walkin' here!'

Smoking

o Forbidden in public spaces, including parks and subway stations, as well as restaurants, bars and taxis.

o Very few hotels have smoking rooms; the majority are smoke-free.

Toilets

o Public restrooms are shamefully scarce. Check crowdsourced map New York Restrooms (www.nyre-stroom.com) for a list.

o Reliable spots are transport hubs (Grand Central, Penn Station), nicer parks (Madison Square Park, Bryant Park and several locations in Central Park) and public libraries. Department stores are a good bet, as are branches of Barnes & Noble.

o Hotel lobby bathrooms work if you're decently dressed.

Tourist Information

NYC Information Center (☎ 212-484-1222; www.nycgo.com; Macy's, 151 W 34th St, at Broadway; ⏰ 10am-10pm Mon-Sat, to 9pm Sun; Ⓢ B/D/F/M, N/Q/R/W to 34th St-Herald Sq)

Visas

o The US Visa Waiver Program (VWP) allows nationals of 38 countries to enter the US without a visa, but you must register with the US Department of Homeland Security and fill out an ESTA application (Electronic System for Travel Authorization; www.cbp. gov/travel/international-visitors/esta). There is a $14 fee. .

o When approved, the registration is valid for two years or until your passport expires, whichever comes first.

o If you hold a passport from a non-VWP country, are staying longer than 90 days or are planning to work or study, you must obtain a visa from a US consulate in your home country.

Behind the Scenes

Send Us Your Feedback

We love to hear from travellers – your comments keep us on our toes and help make our books better. Our well-travelled team reads every word on what you loved or loathed about this book. Although we cannot reply individually to your submissions, we always guarantee that your feedback goes straight to the appropriate authors, in time for the next edition. Each person who sends us information is thanked in the next edition.

Visit **lonelyplanet.com/contact** to submit your updates and suggestions or to ask for help. Our award-winning website also features inspirational travel stories and news. Note: We may edit, reproduce and incorporate your comments in Lonely Planet products such as guidebooks, websites and digital products, so let us know if you are happy to have your name acknowledged. For a copy of our privacy policy visit **lonelyplanet.com/legal**.

Acknowledgements

Cover photograph: Grand Central Station, V_E/Shutterstock ©
Back cover photograph: SoHo building facades, Francois Roux/Shutterstock ©
PAGES 38–9: Ingus Kruklitis/Shutterstock ©, Danor_a/Getty Images ©, Sean Pavone/Shutterstock ©, Cosmin Coita/shutterstock ©, littleny/Getty Images ©

John's Thanks

Thanks to Angela Tinson, Daniel Bolger and my co-author Zora O'Neill. To all the shopkeepers, wait-staff, docents and fellow New Yorkers who answered my questions. Endless love to my partner, Ben Cohen, and my friends. For Erin Garry, my original NYC tour guide.

Zora's Thanks

Much gratitude to my cowriter, John Garry, and to the previous authors of this book. Thanks to Angela Tinson, to Rod Ben Zeev for temporary housing, and to all my neighbors who daily remind me how lucky I am to live in this city.

This Book

This 9th edition of Lonely Planet's Pocket New York City was written by John Garry and Zora O'Neill. The previous edition was written by Ali Lemer, Anita Isalska, MaSovaida Morgan and Kevin Raub.

This guidebook was produced by the following:

Commissioning Editor
Angela Tinson

Product Editor
Gary Quinn

Cartographer
Alison Lyall, Mark Griffith

Book Designer
Dermot Hegarty

Cover Researcher
Gwen Cotter

Thanks to
Hannah Cartmel, Fergal Condon, Shenarri Freeman, Bowen Goh, Mark Griffiths, Charlotte Orr, Katie Trainor

Index

See also separate subindexes for:

⊗ **Eating p253**
⊜ **Drinking p254**
⊕ **Entertainment p254**
⊜ **Shopping p255**

🍸 DRINKING

🎭 Entertainment

🔒 Shopping

Our Writers

John Garry

John Garry is an NYC-based travel journalist and teacher. He grew up in the Catskill Mountains, lived on the Upper West Side for a decade, and spent nearly as long tap dancing across North America and Europe before trading the stage for the page. Brooklyn Heights is his current home, where he writes about everything from art and history to food and nightlife.

Zora O'Neill

Zora O'Neill has lived in New York City (forever and always in the great borough of Queens) since 1998. She has written guidebooks since 2002; for Lonely Planet, she has also covered Amsterdam, Spain, Morocco, Egypt and Greece. She is the author of *All Strangers Are Kin*, a travel memoir about studying Arabic and traveling in the Arab world. See more at www.zoraoneill.com.

Published by Lonely Planet Global Limited
CRN 554153
9th edition - March 2023
ISBN 978 1 83869 192 9
© Lonely Planet 2023 Photographs © as indicated 2023
10 9 8 7 6 5 4 3 2
Printed in Malaysia